# ANGLO-SAXON CHRISTIANITY

# ANGLO-SAXON CHRISTIANITY

Exploring the earliest roots of
Christian spirituality in England

## PAUL CAVILL

**Fount**
*An Imprint of HarperCollinsPublishers*

Fount is an Imprint of
HarperCollins*Religious*
Part of HarperCollins*Publishers*
77–85 Fulham Palace Road, London W6 8JB

First published in Great Britain in 1999 by Fount

© 1999 Paul Cavill

1 3 5 7 9 10 8 6 4 2

Paul Cavill asserts the moral right to be
identified as the author of this work

A catalogue record for this book is
available from the British Library

ISBN 0 00 628112 5

Printed and bound in Great Britain by
Caledonian International Book Manufacturing Ltd, Glasgow

TO SUE

# CONTENTS

# INTRODUCTION

 In May last year I visited Lindisfarne with my family. The island was the base of the Irish mission to Anglo-Saxon Northumbria from the year 635. As we drove up from the busy Midlands, through rush-hour Newcastle, we wondered what to expect. In the region are many famous Anglo-Saxon sites: Bamburgh, a royal fortress; Yeavering, a royal residence, old and important even before the Anglo-Saxons. The monastery on Lindisfarne itself became rich and famous before the vikings took a shine to it. Would there still be anything there to impress or interest my children, who do not generally like 'looking at lumps of stone'?

What we found was an island cut off by the tide. We missed the crossing, and we had to wait five hours before we could get across the causeway to our hosts on the island. Lindisfarne hospitality is freely given, generous and open-handed when you get there, and it always was. But this natural barrier of the sea represents a different kind of barrier. There is a different way of life on the island. It is not cut off from modern life. All the usual technological gadgetry is as much available in Lindisfarne as anywhere else. But the pace of life is different: people walk about, shelves are laden with books, pubs are full of real talk.

While we were there in the bright May sunshine, we wore our coats. The buds of the trees were just cautiously beginning to break open. In the Midlands it was early summer, but on Lindisfarne it was early spring. Within the walled garden, the weather was pleasant, but out by the sea it was still sharp. On the boat trip we took to the Farne Islands, St Cuthbert's famous retreat, the vessel bucked and heaved, and most people were happy to leave the islands to the memory of the saint, to the puffins and seals.

It struck me forcefully that Lindisfarne was wisely chosen by the monks of Iona as their base. It was close enough to the main centres of royal power to allow them to influence the nation. Yet it was cut off by the sea on an unattractive site so that the monks could practise their spiritual life without hindrance or distraction. Its climate and situation enforce discipline and regularity: certain things have to be done at certain times. Hardship and danger from the elements encouraged a longing for the delights of the life of heaven.

But although the monks faced death and disease and focused their whole existence on the spiritual world, they did not seek death. Death when it came was welcome, but life was treasured. Death by neglect was never valued, and was not holy death. Spirituality was not available by default. It had to be worked for by discipline, selflessness, study, labour. Life on Lindisfarne was lived in harmony with the natural world as far as possible. But the inhospitable landscape made hard physical labour necessary, and human company pleasant.

The life developed by the monks on Lindisfarne shaped Anglo-Saxon Christianity to a very large degree. Anglo-Saxon Christianity was never a still backwater of spirituality, but was at the core of the culture, influencing it, and being influenced by it. Anglo-Saxon Christianity bred men and women of quite extraordinary personal holiness, but it never failed to deal with ordinary people as well. In the monasteries the sense of spiritual purpose and the need for physical work combined to give Anglo-Saxon Christianity a hard edge of pragmatism. It was theologically astute and orthodox, borrowing and developing centuries of church tradition. But it asked questions, sought answers, resolved difficulties, opposed errors, sent missions. It taught and cared for people in equal measure. Active and contemplative were two aspects of the same spirituality.

My children found fun on Lindisfarne: good company, some wonderful pictures (from the Lindisfarne Gospels), a break from the ordinariness of life in school and home and church in the city. I think I began to understand Anglo-Saxon Christianity, and why it had attracted and inspired me throughout my first degree in English language and literature and years of research in Old English.

Despite the presence in the literature of strange visions and fantastic miracles, Anglo-Saxon Christianity was more rooted in the life and experience of real people than much of what passes for spirituality today. Spirituality has become a retreat from reality, another world where difficulty can be avoided. A world where the self can be nurtured rather than the soul. A world of sentimentality and 'Celtic' tea towels, manuals of knotwork and do-it-yourself theology. Anglo-Saxon Christianity was a spirituality of the heart: it had passion and commitment to God. A spirituality of the soul: the Anglo-Saxons knew that the soul must be nurtured in worship and service of God. A spirituality of the mind: it valued orthodoxy, learning, literature and poetry, art and music, and saw these as ways of expressing adoration of God.

And a spirituality of the strength, which embraced the physical aspects of human living, all of which could be a response to the goodness and grace of God in providing and sustaining and healing.

This book is an introduction to Anglo-Saxon Christianity. It is not a book on the Anglo-Saxon church, or the history of the evangelization of the English, though of course these come into it. What I have done is read the sources in order to hear what they are saying about life and death, the world and its questions, God and his purposes. I have filled in some of the background, so that even if you know little beyond 1066 *and All That* by W. C. Sellar and R. J. Yeatman, you will be able to see where the Anglo-Saxons got their ideas from.

Some of the stories and texts I have included are well known, others are not. Some of them you might think to be inappropriate for a book on Christianity. But there are all too many *Little Books*, *The Little Book of This*, *The Little Book of That*, which present readers with soundbite-sized platitudes for uncritical acceptance. I want to pay the Anglo-Saxons the basic courtesy of listening to them, and then asking questions. I want to see how they dealt with problems, so the stories and texts are not all of the 'inspirational' type. I give the important texts as near in full as is possible, and I discuss them fully. The texts are at the back of the book so that you can read them and disagree with me if you wish!

Anglo-Saxon Christianity is enchanting, and at times its expression has a loveliness and power beyond compare. In twenty years of teaching (not always very appreciative) students *The Dream of the Rood*, I have never yet seen it fail to produce a spark of interest and enthusiasm. The mute cross speaks still. I hope you will find it so in this book.

# 1

## LIFE AND FAITH IN ANGLO-SAXON NORTHUMBRIA

 What was life like for the Anglo-Saxons? And was there anything about the way they lived and thought that made Christianity particularly attractive? There are several difficulties in the way of giving a simple answer to these questions. For one, the Anglo-Saxon period, from the Conquest of Britain in the fifth century, through to the Norman Conquest of the eleventh, was a very long time; the amount of time since the death of Geoffrey Chaucer to now, or twice as long as there have been English-speaking people in America. For another, the records of Anglo-Saxon England were written by people who might be thought to have a bias towards Christianity. Churchmen, and people with education or status, are generally thought to be somehow insulated from the harshest conditions of life. So they might not be properly in touch with the experience of ordinary people. A third difficulty is that one or two scholars, such as Bede and Alcuin, dominated the intellectual life of early Anglo-Saxon England, and Northumbria in particular. It is all too easy to accept their views as the norm, when they may represent only a small constituency. Finally, the evidence we have from archaeology and literature is at best fragmentary. And it gives very little insight into the feelings of individuals.

So we must ask, 'What of those who had no voice, no way of recording their experience, and no lasting memorial?' Conditions in Anglo-Saxon England varied according to place and time, but some features of life would be fairly constant. To hear these anonymous people, we have to build up a picture from archaeological, literary and historical sources. But without some effort of imagination on our part, they will not engage our sympathy, and we will not understand what Christianity meant to them. So let us go back to the turbulent days of early Northumbria, and imagine what life might have been like in the year 636, in a village in the immemorial hills and deep forests just north and east of the Northumbrian royal estate *Ad Gefrin*, Yeavering, and about the same distance from the king's fortress at *Bebbanburh*, Bamburgh.

## AN ENGLISH VILLAGE

People count the years of the king's reign, so AD 636 is the third year of King Oswald of Northumbria. The village bustles with life, both human and animal: dogs sniffing around, chickens busily pecking at the rubbish. There are both advantages and disadvantages in being so close to the centre of the king's power: you get protection, but you also have to keep the supplies flowing for the king's use. Sometimes the protection fails, too, like the time four years ago when the ancient feud between the Northumbrians and their neighbours to the south and the west, the Mercians and the Welsh, flared up. The Mercian and Welsh armies had attacked Northumbria in retaliation for King Edwin's earlier raids.

Moving to defend his lands, King Edwin had been killed at the battle of Hatfield Chase. Those people who survived told how the enemy armies had split up and gone over the whole country looting, burning and killing in an orgy of revenge.

For ordinary people, like those living in our village, great events repeated in fireside talk and song give a certain brightness to faces and fuel the fierce pride of the men. After the meat and over the mead, in the warmth of companionship, one or another brings out a sword, or a disc of curiously worked bronze with swirling foreign designs, or some other piece of booty, and tells the tale of where it came from and how it was won. The names of great heroes of the past, and their death-defying deeds, trip off the tongue, and the boys know they have great ancestors, and a great deal to live up to. The men know that they are part of a glorious, noble, historical and mythical tradition, stretching back as far as the poets can remember, even as far as the gods. The objects and the weapons are passed from father to son, and the stories with them: that is, if the father does not get killed on campaign, and if the son does not die from disease or the ravages of a raiding party from any of the nearby tribes of Britons. Remembering the years of the king's reign is sometimes difficult; but in this culture, and that of the British, resentment is harboured for generations, even when the origins of the feud can barely be remembered. Kings trace their genealogy back to Woden, god of cunning, war, poetry and drinking, and do not usually fail to inherit the family likeness.

## WORK TO BE DONE

Tales of great deeds take the mind off the drabness of everyday existence. There is always work to be done on the house, where the thatch is leaking or the timbers sinking. In the old days they sacrificed a slave and threw his body into the hole in which they then sank the main timbers of the great hall: a recipe for subsidence, if you like. But even these days timbers slip and sink and split, and it is always at the wrong time: snow, wind and rain wreck houses. There is the constant worry about food. With the forest nearby, there are wild boar, deer, and smaller animals to be caught, and fish in the river. Fruit and nuts and berries make a decent sauce with almost any meat, and leeks and turnips and some green-leaf vegetables can be added to the pot, in season. Most of the domestic animals are killed off at the winter festival, just a good boar and a couple of sows kept for breeding, and they are at risk in a hard winter, as even the horses are. A couple of weeks of rich food, fat and filling, then the long struggle to keep warm and fed. The scent of life of any sort brings the wolves out of the forest in a hard winter, preying, scavenging and carrying off anything edible.

People die in winter. Diseases spread rapidly, cold and hunger take their toll, of beasts as much as people. There are people who remember King Æthelfrith's battle at Chester twenty or more winters ago, but there are not many of them. Some people reach the grand old age of forty, but by then they have lost their teeth, the use of their eyes, and the damp and cold has stiffened their joints so that they can barely move. The arts of hunting are useful in war, indeed it is easier to spear a man than a wily old boar, and the tusks of the boar are just as deadly as the weapons of the warrior. The lads of the upper class are called out for war service by the king from about the age of twelve, and a good proportion of them never make it from the band of the *geoguth*, 'the youth', to the *duguth*, the elite of seasoned warriors. Some are maimed, some killed, some are made slaves.

The women are kept busy with children: feeding and clothing them, teaching them how to do chores. Wool can be traded with the folk who keep sheep on the hills, and has to be spun and woven and dyed. Wood has to be gathered for fires, grain ground for bread, ale brewed, honey collected, berries gathered, animals foddered or taken out to grass, eggs collected. It is hard when you are pregnant, and if you have no slaves or children to help, you risk losing the child in the womb, and your own life in childbirth. As it is, only some of your children survive childhood, and the despair occasionally unhinges the more sensitive women, who refuse their husbands and get a good beating for it.

The king or the king's officials visit every year for tax or on the way to a council or to a war. Unless it is a particularly good year, it means that you go hungry at least some of the time, because the king and his men have to be entertained with the best food and drink. There used to be sacrifices to the gods at the local shrine, for prosperity or success in war, but people are less religious these days. At any rate, the seasonal slaughtering of animals is what has to be done, whether for the gods, the king, or because there is no fodder spare in winter.

## A VISITATION

This year the king visits with a small retinue. As usual, he has his noble thegns, retainers, armed and looking for trouble. But there is a small group of men in dull, simple woollen clothes, with the hair shaved off the front of their heads; this makes them look strange, stranger than slaves even, and the children hide themselves. Both the king and the rest of the shaven men pay particular attention to one of the group. The king's thegns have their horses with them, but neither the king nor the leader of the shaven rides. When they get to the feast, prepared from the best our country can offer, neither the king nor the leader of the shaven eats more than a child's share. Curiously for a warrior king, Oswald seems to prefer to talk quietly with the leader of the shaven in a foreign tongue, rather than join in the bragging and singing. Half way through the celebrations, the king joins all the shaven in singing an entirely different and unheard-of song in another room.

All this is puzzling indeed. The next day, the puzzle remains until the king calls an assembly, not only of the men, but of all the people. In front of all, the leader of the shaven stands up: he is spare, gaunt even, but despite the distance, he exudes power. The king stands with him, and as the leader of the shaven begins to talk in his foreign tongue, the king translates. He speaks of a god, the one true god, powerful and glorious, one who created the earth and all who live on it. This god calls all people to obey him, to honour him as their king, and to worship him as their lord. He says that the old gods are fakes and malicious ones at that, and sacrifices to the great trees and rocks and springs are offensive to the true god, and will be punished. But then the tone softens, and a warmth and gentleness of manner transform the leader of the shaven. He tells of this god's love for people, such that he sent his son as a sacrifice himself to take the punishment for everyone else's wrong-doing. Then to put an end to the feud between himself and the people who killed his son, he made the son come back to life again, and made him king over everything.

The leader of the shaven invites people to join him at the river to take the oath of allegiance to this god, and to show it by being washed in the water. As the request comes through King Oswald, and as his retainers are by now dispersed among the people, of course no one is going to stay at home. But as one or two of the older folk are hobbling along, and as one of the younger men who had been gored and crippled by a boar is being carried, they are helped by the shaven men and even the king himself. In the speech, King Oswald had called the son of this god *hælend*, the saviour and healer. As they are going along, the leader of the shaven turns suddenly to the crippled man, they set him down, and then putting one hand on him and raising the other in the air, the leader of the shaven calls out something. People see with their own eyes the cripple getting up and walking down to the river. As they said afterwards, it was the first time they had really seen a god do anything worthwhile, there and then.

People tend to think of deities in the same way as they think of kings. Some indeed say the gods were kings in the old days when there were giants on the earth, and that they became gods because people believed they could help them. Kings demand things: goods and loyalty and service; but, to be frank, they seldom enough earn them. They take without giving, they are distant, and more often than not absent, when there is a crisis. They have power and can hurt you for no particular reason. You have to be careful with them, appease them, try to curry favour with them. Everyone's name meant something: Æthelfrith meant 'noble peace' or possibly 'noble minded' – the first alternative a bit of a misnomer, most would agree; Edwin meant 'wealth-friend' – closer to the mark; Oswald meant 'god-power' – closer still. Here now was a Healer who had proved his power to do the business. There is a good deal more enthusiasm for the new god now he has proved both his friendship and his power.

# AIDAN AND HIS MONKS

Afterwards, as the shaven men visit periodically, teaching and healing, caring and comforting, people learn that the name of their leader is Aidan. He was one of the men who had taught the faith of Christianity to Oswald in his exile on Iona. As soon as he had gained the kingdom of Northumbria, Oswald had sent for a bishop from Iona to come and teach his people the new faith, which Edwin had embraced before him, but which had been lost in the turmoil following Edwin's death. The good bishop has established a community of the shaven monks on an isolated and windswept island. Actually, not quite an island, but cut off by the sea most of the time. It is known only by the name given it by desperate travellers on the seas in the southerly reaches, *Lindisfarena eg*, 'the island of the travellers from Lindsey', Lindisfarne. These people live in a watery province dominated by the Roman town known as *Lindum colonia*, Lincoln, and if they have to stop off at the island, it must be the last resort.

Not easily convinced even by demonstrations of power, ordinary people are won over by the selfless dedication of the monks. They fear neither bandit nor plague, going unarmed and undefended except for the standard of the cross. They eat little and give much. They own nothing that they call their own, yet they always share what they have. They love women in a way never before known, as people with thoughts and feelings and imagination, rather than as child-bearing drudges. They even seem to have a special relationship with animals, not exploiting them, but treating them with consideration; there are rumours that the wild animals obey them and, in need, even share their food with them. They live for the present, but speak of a future more glorious than anything

imaginable in this life. They are warriors, hardened and used
to fatigue, disciplined, dedicated and utterly loyal to their
lord, yet they serve in the bloodless battle against evil and
ignorance. They avoid strong drink and much food, the usual
preliminaries to song, but sing the most moving and sweet
songs of an ancient king, David by name. Soon, people all over
Northumbria speak of Aidan and his monks with awe and
affection, and many try to follow their way of life: some join
them on Lindisfarne, but there are many other monasteries set
up by the kings and nobility as Christianity takes root.

## COMMUNICATING WITH PEOPLE

This tale of the village folk of Northumbria is fiction, yet it
represents the experience of ordinary people. It shows something of the conditions of life, and the impact of practical
care and holiness on ordinary people. Initially the appeal of
Christianity must have had something to do with *contrast*: the
difference between everyday life and the life lived and taught
by the monks. Later it was to do with the growth of *similarity*
between the highest ideals of secular life and those of
Christianity. This will be explored in the next couple of
chapters. But Christianity in Anglo-Saxon England was never
only a movement of the social and religious elite. It was all-
embracing, speaking the language of the people, Old English,
as well as that of church and state, Latin. It used the script of
the people, runes, as well as the learned Latin alphabet of the
church. It used poetry, prose and pictures, sermon and story.
More effort was made to reach the masses than was seriously
made again until Wesley and Whitefield. And on the human
level, it worked for similar reasons. By and large, those who
preached understood and cared for the people, they went as far

as possible where the people were, and the fruits of their own faith were evident in their lives.

The primary focus of this book is on the Age of Bede, or the Golden Age of Northumbria, as it is often called, from about the middle of the seventh century to the middle of the eighth century. This time was remarkable for a great flowering of scholarship, and for the fairly general peaceableness. It was a time of widespread preaching of the Christian faith and the growth of monasticism: the time after the Anglo-Saxon settlement of British territory and the jostling for supremacy among kings which ensued, and before the time of the viking attacks, which started at the end of the eighth century and dominated much of the rest of Anglo-Saxon history. Some of the products of this time are widely known: the Lindisfarne Gospels; the preaching cross from Ruthwell, near Dumfries in Scotland; the works of Bede himself; Cædmon's *Hymn*. The Anglo-Saxons saw this time of peace as God's blessing on the enterprise of conversion, and set about converting not only the English, but the people of the ancient Germanic homelands, Germany and Frisia.

The history and art of the Age of Bede is striking in many ways, but you cannot help noticing perhaps most of all how *articulate* it is. The Ruthwell Cross preaches in many different 'languages': pictures, English runes, and Latin; in prose and verse; in scripture and Christian story. A comb recovered from Anglo-Saxon Whitby has an inscription combining Old English and Latin, all written in runic letters, 'my God, God almighty, help Cy[...]'. The Lindisfarne Gospels reveal in their decoration a conception of the mysteriousness and intricacy of the message they contain, familiar yet always unfathomed. Here is a vocabulary of ornament and script which articulates wonders. Communication was a serious enterprise, carried on at different levels by many means.

# PERSONAL AND POPULAR

Christianity, however established, political, adapted to social conditions, superficial – and it was, on occasion, all these in Anglo-Saxon England – is and always has been a faith that embraces and affects the whole person. It engages heart, soul, mind and strength. Closing his monumental *Ecclesiastical History of the English People* in the year 731, having listed most of his books, Bede wrote this prayer:

> And I pray you, good Jesus, that since you have gra-
> ciously given me your words of knowledge sweetly
> to drink, so also you will grant in friendship that I
> might come finally to you, the fount of all wisdom,
> and remain forever in your presence.

Bede was the foremost scholar of his age. His *History* tells us a little about him, how he was born on the estate of the monastery at Wearmouth-Jarrow, was entrusted to the monastery at the age of seven, and devoted himself to a life of learning and teaching. His prayer reflects his love of scholarship and his joy at the prospect of being with his Lord, forever thirsty and forever drinking of the fountain of divine wisdom. This image brings us closer to the heart of the man: humble, warm, sincere. But such intimacy is rare in Anglo-Saxon sources: we have a few letters, but nothing like the journals and writings which illuminate the spiritual development of Margery Kempe, or Julian of Norwich. Often we have, as it were, to look *through* the objective discourse of scholars to see their personal motivation and passion.

Bede's *Life of Saint Cuthbert* gives us a tantalizing glimpse of the reaction of some ordinary people to monks in difficulty on rafts near the mouth of the Tyne. The rafts were drifting out to sea, and a crowd had gathered watching:

> They began to jeer at their way of common life, as if anyone were deserving of this kind of suffering for spurning the ordinary usages of human beings and introducing new and strange rules of living. Cuthbert put a stop to the abuse of the mockers, saying, 'What are you doing, brothers, slandering people who are even now being carried off to destruction? Wouldn't it be better and more humane to pray to the Lord for them to be saved rather than finding pleasure in their perils?' But, crude in mind and words, they contradicted him, 'No one should plead for them, and God should not have mercy on them, because they have taken away the old ways of worship, and nobody knows how the new worship should be carried out.' When he got this response, Cuthbert knelt down with his head bowed to the ground, and prayed to God, and immediately the strong wind shifted and blew the rafts undamaged back to land ... Seeing this, the people were embarrassed at their unbelief. (Chapter 3)

These people are given a voice by Bede, in his enchanting *Life*. They express their fear of the unknown, their resistance to change, and their resentment against those who apparently set themselves apart. Yet Cuthbert is there, staking a claim for kindness and compassion, and sticking his neck out (quite literally) on behalf of both monks and people. He sees opposition as opportunity, not threat. And the people have the grace to respond to him, and through him to a God who does something to help.

# SOURCES

Our imaginary village scene and the episode from Bede's *Life of Saint Cuthbert* given above, reflect the repeated, almost insistent, testimony of the literary sources about the reception of Christianity. The element of miracle is consistently present, as it is in many more stories given below. Reconstructing the history of the times omitting the miraculous is almost impossible. Making due allowance for a pre-scientific world view and pious convention among the Anglo-Saxons, there nevertheless remain events and developments which defy rational explanation. To dismiss these things out of hand, as many do, can be mere intellectual laziness. On the other hand, I am not sure that we can responsibly accept everything the Anglo-Saxon sources tell us.

I take a relatively critical stance towards Bede's stories, much as I love them. Bede is one of the few writers who took pains to collect, identify and verify his sources. His mind was disciplined and creative. He arranged his material in such a way as to make the greatest impact. When he rewrote the *Life of Saint Cuthbert* by an anonymous monk of Lindisfarne, he added material (the story above does not appear in the anonymous *Life*) and corrected errors. In other words, he engaged with his material, and saw it as his responsibility to tease out the significance of it. Bede's stories and the other material in this book are now our sources, and we should no more accept them uncritically than Bede did his.

These sources merit attention and reflection, not simply acceptance; their value to us is as much in their ability to make us think and question our own understanding, as in their inspiring examples and illustrations of commitment and perseverance. Moreover, as I shall try to show, Anglo-Saxon

Christianity as a whole adopted a position of pragmatism which consistently sought to reconcile contrasting, if not opposing, views, while retaining a firm grasp on matters of central importance. It saw no significant distinction between spirituality and involvement in the world. It was a humane, life-affirming, conscientious and spiritual faith, able to acknowledge differences of opinion while respecting the achievements of, and giving value to, those who held different opinions. In its grasp of the notion of the unity of all Christians in Christ, it resolved some of the problems of secular tribalism. And in these days of renewed secular and religious and indeed Christian tribalism, the Anglo-Saxon church gives a lead in its assertion of true unity and unity in truth.

# 2

## CONVERSION, LIFE AND DEATH

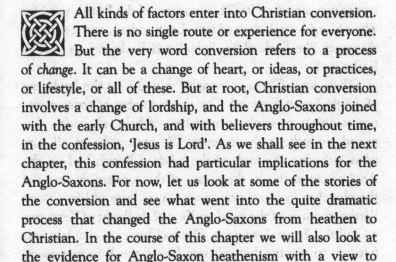

All kinds of factors enter into Christian conversion. There is no single route or experience for everyone. But the very word conversion refers to a process of *change*. It can be a change of heart, or ideas, or practices, or lifestyle, or all of these. But at root, Christian conversion involves a change of lordship, and the Anglo-Saxons joined with the early Church, and with believers throughout time, in the confession, 'Jesus is Lord'. As we shall see in the next chapter, this confession had particular implications for the Anglo-Saxons. For now, let us look at some of the stories of the conversion and see what went into the quite dramatic process that changed the Anglo-Saxons from heathen to Christian. In the course of this chapter we will also look at the evidence for Anglo-Saxon heathenism with a view to understanding how it shaped the response of the people to Christianity.

## CHRISTIAN MISSIONS

The Germanic warriors who invaded and settled Britain in the fifth century were heathen. Yet within just three hundred years, by the middle of the eighth century, Northumbria was the powerhouse of Christianity in Europe outside Rome. England was now sending its missionaries out to Germanic territories on the continent and elsewhere. This conversion was the result of several remarkable missionary enterprises. Perhaps most remarkable of all was that it was accomplished without a single martyrdom, and without enforced conversion. Missionaries came from various parts, from Gaul (modern France), Rome, and Iona-Lindisfarne. And there were pockets of Christian believers remaining among the British populace whose continuing faithfulness is obliquely recorded in place-names containing *eccles*. This is a form of the British word for 'church', *egles*, itself derived from Latin *ecclesia*, and it survives in names like Egglescliffe, Exhall and Eccleston, as well as Eccles itself.

There were Christian remains dotted over the landscape of Anglo-Saxon England. The sheer number of *eccles* place-names points to small communities of believers widely dispersed throughout the country. We cannot be at all sure what influence the faith of the subdued British had on the Anglo-Saxons. But in the course of the conversion, many of the churches in Kent were given a new lease of life. Queen Bertha, the wife of the heathen King Æthelberht of Kent, was a Gaulish Christian princess. She had her own chaplain and freedom to practise her religion, before the Roman mission even arrived. The base of the mission became the Roman church of St Martin, a Gaulish saint famous in Britain, at which Bertha was accustomed to pray. Reading between the lines, it seems likely that there was spiritual work being done among the Anglo-Saxons before the formal missions.

Bede's *Ecclesiastical History* gives prominence to the Roman mission, which brought a party of missionaries to

English shores in 597. But a lot of what Bede writes also testifies to the importance of the Irish missionaries from Lindisfarne, whose work of conversion was more significant than that of the Roman mission, in the north of England at least. As far as Bede was concerned, these were the two most significant influences on Anglo-Saxon Christianity: Rome and Ireland. And within seventy-odd years of the beginning of Christian mission, the English church was independent enough to decide which of the significant influences on its development should be affirmed and which rejected. This choice, taken at the Council of Whitby, was to be a painful one, and the issues will be discussed in a later chapter. But the stories of the conversion itself are joyful. The most picturesque ones come from Bede. But Bede makes the most of stories that were more widely known: the account of Gregory's punning was known to a monk of Whitby who wrote a Life of Pope Gregory early in the eighth century before Bede wrote his *History*. We turn now to these stories and then go on to consider what we can learn of the heathenism which was replaced by Christianity.

## GREGORY'S ANGELS (TEXT 1)

The first stirring of a desire to evangelize the Anglo-Saxons came to Gregory, later to be Pope Gregory the Great, in the market at Rome, some time after the year 560. He saw some slaves with fair hair for sale, and asked about them. Told that they were Angles from the island of Britain, who were still heathen, he clearly saw God's guidance in the answers, as he punned on the words. 'Angles' he associated with 'angels'. 'Deira', the kingdom where they came from, with their rescue 'from wrath' (*de ira* in Latin). And the name of their king,

'Ælle', he associated with 'alleluia' and the praise of God. This kind of word-association shows a lightness of touch, a pleasure in the coincidences of life and language, the falling together of things not otherwise linked. But it is also serious. Medieval biblical interpretation (as we shall see later) has a delight in such things. One of the most influential books of the entire Middle Ages, Isidore of Seville's *Etymologies*, is based very substantially on this kind of association of words and ideas. Underlying it is the sense that with God nothing is coincidental. So it was for Gregory, and as soon as he became Pope, he put into action a plan for the conversion of the Angles.

The man chosen for the job was Augustine, later St Augustine of Canterbury, and quite a different person from St Augustine of Hippo the great writer and Father of the fifth century. Trekking across half of Europe, Augustine and his little band had more than a few misgivings about their task. Bede describes them as terror-stricken at the prospect of preaching to 'a barbarous, savage, and unbelieving people, whose language they did not know' (Text 2). They wrote a tentative letter to Gregory, suggesting that it might be a good idea to give up such a dangerous task. But Gregory insisted they carry on. So, doubtless with heavy hearts, they persevered.

They arrived in Thanet in 597, and were immediately provided for by King Æthelberht, whose wife was a Christian (Text 3). Then Æthelberht arranged to meet the delegation, in the open air, lest they should put a spell on him. The missionaries approached him carrying a silver cross as a standard, and a painted panel with the image of a king on it, and singing a Latin hymn. It is impossible to read the account of this meeting without seeing that Æthelberht was the one who was afraid. And the missionaries must have made an impression of power and authority with their standard and image. However little Æthelberht had investigated his wife's faith, he knew, of course, that her relatives were powerful people, and that they owed allegiance to Rome. So he knew he had to be careful. Conceding nothing but an acknowledgement that their message sounded fair enough, he nevertheless gave them freedom to preach. Later he allowed them to use as their base the Roman church of St Martin in Canterbury.

The life of the missionaries in Canterbury was monastic: disciplined, simple and regular. The missionaries preached with power and relevance, and worked miracles to prove the message (Text 4). The king himself was baptized in due course, and like the Emperor Constantine before him, encouraged the faith with his patronage. All kinds of issues cropped up, and the correspondence between Augustine and Gregory is full of practical problems which needed to be resolved. Bede had the papal archives in Rome searched for his information on the Roman mission, and he gives us the letters pretty well in full. In one of them, Gregory wrote to Augustine warning him, quite severely, not to let miracles go to his head, but to see them as God's provision (Text 5). Another of the issues was precisely what attitude the mission should take towards the heathen religion. The letter Gregory wrote on this occasion has proved to be of immense significance in interpreting the conversion, both then and more recently.

Gregory wrote to Abbot Mellitus with a message for Augustine telling him to embrace as much as possible of the habitual practice of the Anglo-Saxons and turn it to good Christian purpose (Text 6). So Augustine was not to destroy heathen shrines or try to force the people to stop their sacrifices. Rather he was to adapt heathen sites to Christian uses and help the people to worship the true God when they sacrificed their animals. As people whose lives had been formed by monastic discipline, Gregory and Augustine knew that habit could just as well be good and enabling as otherwise.

This letter captures the flavour of early English Christianity and testifies to Gregory's personal influence over the subsequent development of Christianity in England. It is intensely pragmatic, recognizing the importance of habit and the principle of fairness of exchange. It is absolutely clear at the level of religious conviction, seeing heathen worship, as do many biblical and other writers, as worship of devils. Yet it distinguishes between action and belief, seeing it as possible that the same actions can be motivated by completely opposite belief-systems. Strangely, this and other evidence has been interpreted to imply that Christianity was syncretistic, and that if we look at it closely we will see the blending and mingling of heathen and Christian elements. But the more closely and critically we look at the literature, the less syncretistic Anglo-Saxon Christianity appears.

## ANGLO-SAXON HEATHENISM

Such was the effectiveness of the conversion, and the radical nature of the break with what went before in religious terms, that it is extremely difficult to find out what *did* go before. Some scholars resort to the expedient of putting Anglo-Saxon heathenism alongside Scandinavian mythology. The theory is that they were both Germanic and therefore they will represent the same beliefs. But the earliest written records of Scandinavian mythology come from about four centuries later than the great thrust of English conversion. A notable facet of Scandinavian religion, according to recent work on the subject, was its sheer variability. Scandinavian heathenism had no doctrine as such, and hence could have no heresy. It was a clutch of local practices, traditions, symbols and stories. We know a little about the gods and sacrifices in Anglo-Saxon England, but any coherent system of belief beyond that is elusive.

Many times in the sermon literature and in the decrees of kings and councils, heathenism is prohibited, especially worship of whatever kind at wells, trees and stones. There are some associations between these natural features and worship of heathen gods in the Scandinavian sources. Most of the distinctively heathen place-names of England are also associated with natural features, but surprisingly few of them are these particular ones. Groves are the most commonly represented, with Wensley, Thundersley and Thursley. Here the name of the gods, Woden and Thunor, is combined with the Old English word for a clearing in a wood, a grove, *leah*. This naming pattern ties in with what Tacitus says about the Germanic nations on the continent, that 'their holy places are woods and groves'. There is very little to tie worship of the heathen gods in with these Christian prohibitions. It looks more probable that a kind of ill-defined animism was the major and lasting threat to Christianity rather than Wodenism or worship of the other heathen gods. It also looks as if the writers did not really know what went on among the people, and therefore resorted to a traditional formula which covered more or less anything that was not Christian.

Bede wrote of the conversion of King Sigeberht of East Anglia. He describes that king being persuaded of the folly of idol-worship by his Christian friend Oswiu, king of Northumbria. No god could be made of wood or stone, the other bits of which could be burnt or thrown away, Oswiu argued. Clear evidence, we might think, that Anglo-Saxon heathenism involved idol images, as various sources tell us

Scandinavian heathenism did. This is not improbable, as there are many other references to idol worship in Bede and elsewhere. But it is just as likely that the story arises out of biblical polemic against idolatry. In Isaiah 44, for example, a man cuts down a tree and from one bit of it he makes an idol to worship, and with the remainder he makes a fire to keep himself warm and to bake his bread. The similarities suggest that the story of King Oswiu's discussions has undergone reshaping to reflect the Bible more closely.

## SACRIFICES AND RUNES

Christianity brought the technology of writing, but Christians recorded almost nothing of heathenism. When Bede records the seasonal festivals of the heathen Anglo-Saxons, about the raciest thing he tells us is that they had one called *modranecht*, 'the night of mothers'. It is a reasonable guess that this was not the equivalent of Mother's Day. But there is more than a suspicion that Bede knew no – or very little – more than we do. He also mentions *Eosturmonath*, the month named after the goddess of the dawn, Eostre, Christianized to Easter, and the early winter festival, *Blotmonath*, 'the month of sacrifice', among others. But beyond the fact that animals were sacrificed, he tells us almost nothing. The sacrifices could have been no more than the slaughtering of animals that could not be kept over the winter for food.

The script that the Germanic nations had before vellum, ink and the Latin alphabet, namely runes, was one designed to be carved or scratched into wood, stone or other hard materials. Its origins go back into the early centuries of our era, but apart from inscriptions which are difficult to interpret, nothing in England suggests the elaborate magical functions of runes so beloved of fantasists. Runic letters representing English sounds were adopted into the predominantly Roman alphabet of the English church, and were used as normal letters or abbreviations in ordinary writing. The prayer on the Whitby comb is in runic letters, and St Cuthbert's coffin and the Ruthwell cross have runic inscriptions. One very curious use of runes is in the Old English poetic dialogue between Solomon, who anachronistically represents Christianity, and Saturn, who represents heathenism. They ask each other hard questions to see which of them is the wisest. Solomon the Christian talks of the 'golden word of God', the words of power which work wonders. He then gives the first letters of the Latin Lord's Prayer, PATER NOS, in runes (Text 7).

## CHARMS

Some of the Anglo-Saxon charms, especially those in verse, probably originated in pre-Christian times. One of the few references to Woden is found in one of them, the *Nine Herbs Charm* (Text 8). It aligns herbs such as mugwort, plantain, fennel and chervil against poisons of various sorts, then there is a striking narrative passage:

> A snake came writhing, and it bit a man.
> Then Woden took nine glory-twigs,
> and struck the serpent so that it fell into nine parts.

The narrative is intended to reinforce by mythological precedent the power of the herbs and the charm as a whole. Scandinavian sources associate Woden with healing wisdom, and more particularly with the number nine, and it is possible that there is genuine heathen tradition here. But towards the end of the metrical part of the *Nine Herbs Charm*, before the 'doctor's' claim to authority and the prose instructions on how to use the herbs, there is the line,

> Christ stood over disease of every kind.

This is one of the very few examples of syncretism in Old English literature. The more usual attitude to the heathen gods was to see them as delusions of the devil. The *Maxims* poem puts it very simply, echoing Psalm 95:5 and 1 Chronicles 16:26:

> Woden made idols, the Ruler of All
> created glory, the spacious skies.

It is perhaps to be expected that we will get a biased picture of heathenism from Christian literature. Piecing together all the sources, heathenism was not a coherent system of belief. It was rather a collection of traditions and superstitions that validated the habitual practices of the people, and tried to control the terror people felt in times of disease and death. The missionaries must have been struck by the relevance of the words of the biblical writer to the Hebrews, who described the purpose of Jesus thus:

> he shared in their humanity so that by his death he
> might destroy him who holds the power of death – that
> is, the devil – and free those who all their lives were
> held in slavery by their fear of death.

# LIFE AND DEATH

Charms are the literature of desperation. Ideas from any source, which might give hope to the suffering, found a place. Other charms have strings of 'magical' gobbledegook, meaningless syllables, bits of Latin, instructions on ritual actions such as culling herbs at dawn, crossing rivers and keeping silent – anything to enhance the air of mystery and lend authority to the charmer. These things apparently co-existed with a predominantly Christian world view. Sometimes Christian mumbo-jumbo has replaced heathen elements. But even Christian and classical learning had little to add to help the ill. A Latin medical treatise called the *Medicina de Quadrupedibus* is, unusually, found in a number of Anglo-Saxon manuscripts, including two translations into Old English. A number of its prescriptions involve the medicinal use of dog's excrement or vomit (Text 9). It is impossible to say whether these recipes ever became common practice, but they certainly became part of the stock of Anglo-Saxon learning, as is shown by the number of copies there are of the text. And I could not give an opinion as to the medical properties of the ingredients; but to modern eyes the cure looks a good deal worse than the ailment.

Desperation in the face of debilitating disease and death is the underlying theme of these recipes. One of the main contributing factors was famine. The *Anglo-Saxon Chronicle* is dotted with references to bad harvests, disease of cattle and undefined plagues, which wiped out large numbers of people. The *Maxims* poem says simply,

> The one who eats too seldom becomes sick; though you
>     put him in the sun
> he cannot live on the weather, even if it is warm in the
>     summer.
> He will be overcome prior to death, if he does not know
>     how to sustain life with food.
> Strength is fed by food.

And if there is no food, you die. In the early days after the
conversion, the sources repeatedly refer to apostasy in times of
famine and plague.

The Anglo-Saxons practised both inhumation (burial) and
cremation, and while it is not unusual for grave goods to
accompany cremation burials, inhumation burials generally
furnish more evidence about the conditions of life. The overall
picture from the skeletons would suggest that it was relatively
unusual for people to live over forty years, and that it was common for children to die young. Skeletons show wounds and
deformities of various kinds, including particularly the results
of osteoarthritis, and according to recent evidence, leprosy and
tuberculosis, among many other less identifiable diseases.

This complements the evidence of the literature, which
suggests that it was unusual for an Anglo-Saxon king to die
in his bed at an advanced age. A conventional figure in Old
English poetry is the woman lamenting at the funeral pyre of
her menfolk. But a slightly different tone, one which has an
edge of despair along with its fatalistic acceptance of death,
can be heard in the quirky, proverbial *Maxims* poem:

> The one ready to depart must go, the doomed man must
>     die
> and every day struggle against his separation from

the earth. The ordaining Lord alone knows
where the plague goes, that departs from our land.
He adds children where early death takes away,
so that there are just as many people on earth;
there would be no limit to the population
if he who made the world did not diminish it.

Christianity did not immediately change the world of the Anglo-Saxons where such things happened. The poet tries to find a purpose in his faith for it all, and by over-compensating for the devastation of loss, reveals how close to the quick it cuts.

## VISION

A keynote of the conversion is the emphasis on vision. Many of the miracles that are recorded of personal conversion include angelic visitors, visions of heaven and hell, healing of blind people, and indeed, punitive blinding of persecutors. Bede tells the story of the early British martyr, St Alban, whose executioner's eyes dropped out as soon as he had beheaded the saint. In an attempt to persuade the British bishops to join him in converting the English, St Augustine arranged a miracle competition (Text 10). Whoever could heal a blind man would be right about that particular issue. The British bishops were unable to help, where Augustine healed the man. Since the man was English, the miracle signifies Augustine's role in enlightening the Anglo-Saxons, and it falls into place with all the other proofs of God's blessing on Augustine's mission.

The prominence in Bede's writings of miracles relating to being blind or blinded and seeing suggests that 'seeing the light' was as powerful a metaphor for conversion then as it was in the days of Newton or Wesley. The image captures the duality of conversion. Faith has an impact on very physical things. The pragmatic Anglo-Saxons could see that faith worked, that it changed people and relationships. They saw miracles, too, that made a difference to life. But faith also changes the *way* people see, opening up a whole new world of glory and hope beyond what can be seen physically.

A tender and moving passage in the *Maxims* speaks of the misery of blindness.

> Happy is the innocent in heart. The blind man is deprived of his eyes,
> – clear vision is taken from him – they cannot see the stars bright in the sky,
> or the sun and moon. That is painful to him in his mind,
> a source of anxiety because he alone knows what it is like, and he expects no change.
> The Lord ordained that suffering for him, and he can grant him relief,
> healing for the eye, if he knows him to be pure in heart.

The poet is trying to come to terms with suffering and loss. The vignette of the blind man starts and ends with Matthew 5:8, 'Blessed are the pure in heart; for they will see God.' Within that context, the poet fully enters into the blind man's misery: the beauty he cannot see, the isolation and self-doubt that his affliction causes. Then the poet goes on to refer to the story of the healing of the man born blind in John 9:1–12. In this gospel passage, there is a debate among Jesus' disciples as to why the man was blind, which Jesus resolves with the words, 'this happened so that the work of God might be displayed in his life', and promptly heals the man. The *Maxims* passage is rooted in the conviction that even blindness can be healed here and now, if God so wishes. Both condition and remedy are in his hands. And if healing is not to be, then there is the promise that the pure in heart shall see God, a prospect of greater glory than seeing sun, moon or stars. The poet reflects the hope and consolation that the Bible gives, with not a shred of pious platitude.

# THE CONVERSION DEBATE IN KING EDWIN'S HALL (TEXT 11)

The best story of conversion is Bede's account of the council in which King Edwin accepted the new faith. No story better shows how Christianity appealed equally to the pragmatist and the visionary.

Paulinus, one of Augustine's missionary band, has been preaching in Northumbria, and by giving a sign which Edwin had seen in dream, has convinced Edwin to become a Christian. The king then holds a council to consult his men, and asks what they think of the new religion. In the story Coifi, the high priest of the heathen religion, becomes the advocate of Christianity, because, he says, he has not got much benefit from his own devotion. Another of the king's councillors displays a yearning for secure knowledge about the after-life and the eternal realm, likening human life to a sparrow flying through a warm hall on a dark wintry evening: 'If this new religion tells us more about what is outside the hall, then we should accept it,' he says. With the support and agreement of all, Coifi rides off to desecrate the heathen shrine he had earlier consecrated. Christianity wins the argument from two angles: it works as heathenism does not, and it teaches definite things about the unknown world beyond the grave.

Recent scholars have examined this story in detail and shown how little of it can be verified from other sources. It is perhaps the cumulative effect of the detail that makes us instinctively want to believe it. Bede gives us names and places, believable characters, horses and weapons, the reaction of the people. Narrative competence and coherence is of course no disproof of historical truth. But look at how Bede puts the reflective, delicate image of the sparrow in the councillor's speech between the hard-headed, down-to-earth, materialistic speeches of Coifi, to show the appeal of Christianity across the spectrum of personalities. Then consider how quickly Coifi has acquired the theological vocabulary of salvation. And observe the analytical world view and discourse of truth and knowledge in religion that both Coifi and the unnamed councillor express. And finally see how Coifi adopts a biblical pattern of behaviour in destroying the idols he formerly worshipped: compare for example Gideon. Here is a story which Christians could understand and set within their own world view; but as a historical account of the conversion of Northumbria, it begins to look a little suspect.

Apart from the picturesque details, this story gives two positive pieces of information about heathen belief. One is that it lacked any doctrine of the after-life, and the other is that its high priests were not allowed to bear arms or ride stallions. Edwin's council was held in 627. At about the same time some one hundred and fifty miles to the south east, a ship, weapons, food, money and all the everyday requirements of noble living, were buried in a mound at Sutton Hoo. It may be that the burial and grave goods were just extravagant expressions of grief and lavish display of wealth. Since the spoons in the ship have *Paulos* and possibly *Saulos* inscribed in Greek on them, they may have been baptismal gifts. And if the person commemorated by the ship-burial was baptized, it would suggest that the mode of burial was a matter of tradition rather than conviction. But the burial does suggest that pre-Christian religion had some notions of the after-life, in which a man might need such things.

Some burials include tools for woodworking and other trades. A man's trade will not die out when he himself dies, and tools do not cease to be useful and valuable to other craftsmen, but the deceased might need the tools on 'the other side'. But wherever Bede got the story of the sparrow from, we cannot fully credit the notion that heathenism had no concept of life before birth and after death. The statement of the councillor owes more to a Christian understanding of the limitations of heathenism than to genuine heathen tradition. But the man's quest for 'more certain information' is believable: he is looking for a reasonable basis for faith.

The other piece of information relating to the taboos surrounding a heathen high priest seems more reliable. Official occasions and official meeting-places traditionally excluded weapons. There is some evidence for stallions having cultic significance through being fertility symbols, which might explain the priest of the cult being forbidden to ride them. The throwing of the spear into the sanctuary is widely thought to be the equivalent of the throwing of a spear over an enemy to dedicate them to Woden and destruction. All these things are suggestive and could well be genuine tradition. But whether Bede or his audience understood what we believe to be their heathen significance must remain questionable.

Perhaps it is unduly sceptical to conclude so, but at best Bede is preserving and improving a tradition of the conversion of King Edwin, using all his considerable story-telling skills. At worst, he is covering up a more violent confrontation between organized heathenism and the forces of Christianity in seventh-century Northumbria by making up or elaborating the story of Coifi's zeal, and the councillor's wistfulness. Possibly Bede needed an explanation of the conversion which allowed a benign interpretation of the burning down of shrines. Since Coifi was not one of the missionaries, his violent action in destroying the shrines would fall outside Pope Gregory's general instructions to the mission to preserve heathen places of worship for Christian use. And since Coifi was the high priest he presumably had the authority to do such things. There are, moreover, other less memorable accounts of the conversion of King Edwin, including one which attributes the work to Celtic missionaries rather than Roman ones, a possibility which Bede may have wished to deny.

But the verifiable fact remains that the king received baptism on Easter Day in the year of our Lord 627, and Northumbria became, at least for the duration of Edwin's reign, Christian. That was undoubtedly what was most significant to Bede and his readers. They would hear in the councillor's image of the sparrow the sound of their own yearning for spiritual security in an uncertain and painful world. And they would hear in the hard-headedness of Coifi their own rejection of meaningless ritual and their demand that religion should make practical sense. Christianity answered both needs.

# 3

## CULTURE AND FAITH: ASSIMILATION OR CONFRONTATION?

One of the fundamental claims of Christianity is that it is relevant to people everywhere because it is true. This can be dismissed as cultural imperialism, and certainly Christians have been guilty of demanding conformity in culturally unnecessary and irrelevant matters. But Christianity cannot be abstract. It has to be embodied within cultures because people live within cultures. In this sense it is impossible to recreate 'New Testament Christianity' because the culture of the New Testament world was different from ours, and culture forms and conditions the ways we think and believe and act. There has to be a constant negotiation between culture and faith, with give and take on both sides. So some things in Anglo-Saxon Christianity may be slightly shocking or distasteful to the modern mind; but it is probably a good idea to remind ourselves that there is much in modern Christianity that would be shocking and distasteful to the Anglo-Saxons. This might help us better see where we have identified our cultural assumptions with Christianity.

English people like to believe, in the words of the popular song of the Second World War, that 'There'll always be an England'; many of us apparently believe that there *has always been* an England. Because many of us live in it and take it for granted, we tend to be uncritical, if not uninformed, about our land and its culture. We have generally only the haziest notions about the origins of England, and the influences from all over the world which have since had their part in creating its cosmopolitan society. Christianity has had a massive influence on England and the English. Reading and writing, the Latin alphabet and classical literature, historical, philosophical and scientific enquiry, building in stone and musical notation, are but a few of the huge range of familiar non-religious elements of our cultural heritage which all came with Christianity to England within the early years following the conversion. Much more followed later.

In the course of time, Anglo-Saxon Christianity adapted itself to some aspects of the dominant Germanic culture and changed others. Some aspects of culture were assimilated and made Christian, others were resisted. Certain parts of the culture were more hospitable to some Christian ideas and resisted others. It is stimulating to see how a different age negotiated the relationship between its culture and Christian faith. In this chapter we will look at what the Anglo-Saxons brought with them when they invaded Britain, and what happened to the culture when they became Christian.

## ORIGINS (TEXT 12)

In AD 98, Tacitus wrote about the continental Germanic tribes in his *Germania*. These tribes were the ancestors of the Angles, Saxons and Jutes who were later to invade Britain. An excellent anthropological work, the *Germania* first outlines the general characteristics of the Germanic peoples, then fills in details of each tribe. Tacitus writes of the characteristic organization of Germanic men into warbands. The chief was leader by virtue of his personal prowess, and he gathered men around him not only by his reputation, but also by generous dispensing of the spoils of war to his warriors. Every battle was not only a means of gaining spoils and honour, but also a practical reinforcement of the loyalty between chief and retainer. The renown attached to the chief, the chief rewarded his followers.

Predatory warfare had become institutionalized, the norm, among the Germanic tribes. Indeed, Tacitus tells us that they preferred the quick rewards of warfare to the hard slog of agriculture. The focus of the Germanic ethos was personal: loyalty to one's chief and loyalty to one's family. That loyalty extended even to marriage, and Tacitus observed that adultery was extremely rare among the Germanic tribes. Long after Tacitus, it was members of the Germanic tribes, with a recognizably similar culture to their earlier fellows, who invaded and settled Britain.

The Angles, Saxons and Jutes came to Britain from the north-western seaboard of Europe: from the area of the Jutland peninsula (now Denmark) in the north, down through the area of modern northern and central Germany, through the Netherlands, to the northern parts of modern France in the south. And they came much as they had come when their predecessors were in the pay of the Roman Empire, and indeed as they had come on sundry occasions when opportunity for casual piracy offered. The sea-route used by the invaders was the same as had been used by soldiers, traders and raiders before.

The particular tract of land we call England now, bounded by Scotland to the north and Wales and Ireland to the west, and Europe beyond the Channel to the south and east, has not been forever England. The Anglo-Saxons called the land they came to in the fifth century *Brytene*, a form of the Roman *Britannia*. The Britons were of Celtic stock and had been conquered, Christianized and civilized by the Romans. Britannia had been a Roman colony for four hundred years, but the last legions had left early in the fifth century when Rome itself was under threat from Germanic invaders. The terrible irony is that, according to the tradition, the Roman British king Vortigern invited Germanic warriors to fight for him as mercenaries against the savage Celtic Picts in AD 449. Rome took her legions back to fight against Germanic invaders, Roman Britain invited Germanic invaders to fight against Celtic raiders.

The Germanic Angles and Saxons were dramatically successful. Moreover they saw an opportunity for themselves, and, inviting their kinsmen over on their own account, started to take over the civilized and not terribly well-defended country. The relative efficiency of the Roman Empire's administration and army had restrained the excesses of opportunism before, but now there was nothing to prevent a new outpost of the growing Germanic Empire being assembled from the fractured pieces left behind at Rome's departure.

Within two hundred years, by about the end of the seventh century, the vast majority of what had been Roman Britain was Anglo-Saxon England. It was divided into historically varying numbers of small kingdoms. Very broadly, the Angles settled the northern and eastern parts of Britain, including lowland Scotland, the Saxons the southern and western parts, and the Jutes concentrated mostly on Kent. The Celtic people were now called *wealhas*, Welsh, a word which has various meanings in Anglo-Saxon from 'foreigners' to 'persons of inferior status, slaves'. The country was now *Angelcynna lond*, the land of the English race, and ultimately *Englaland*, the land of the English, and it was probably as accurate then as it is now: which is, not very. There were stretches of the country which were still Celtic: large parts of the south west, and some parts of the north west. The borders were unstable for much of the six hundred years of Anglo-Saxon hegemony. But the initial changes would have been obvious to an observer: some devastation of the old Roman estates; new farms created, new buildings in wood, new social structures, a new heathen religion, a new language; an entire new culture.

## CULTURE AND LANGUAGE

It would be hard to pinpoint an area of life in which the Anglo-Saxons were more advanced culturally than the Britons. That they had some advantages in the arts of war is obvious. But there is an element of wonderment in the reaction of the Anglo-Saxons to some of the abilities of the Britons. Their stone buildings the Anglo-Saxons called *enta geweorc*, the work of giants, because the Anglo-Saxons did not build with stone, only timber. And the Britons had some areas of knowledge and power that the Anglo-Saxons had to borrow a word for – they practised *dry-cræft*, magic in general, and magic associated with druids in particular. For all that, the Anglo-Saxons borrowed little from the Britons by way of language, a few place-names, mostly relating to physical features like hills (*bre* and *pen*), and not much more.

Land and nation had some significance for the Germanic peoples, but not as much as warband and family. Their names reflect this. England, the land of the Angles, ends where English power ends, not at a point on a map or even, in the early stages, at a boundary marker. An early stratum of place-names contains the *-ing-*, *-inga-* elements which means basically the settlement 'of the people of X', where X is often a chieftain's name. Nottingham in its early form meant 'the settlement of the family or followers of a man called Snot' (the S of Snot's name having been lost in early Middle English). The settlement was made by Snot and his men or his descendants, and if they were the original Anglo-Saxon settlers, then they probably gained the land by force from the former Celtic inhabitants.

## A CELTIC VIEW (TEXT 13)

Tacitus gives a benign picture of the Germanic people that he saw. His picture of the noble Germanic savages was intended at least in part to shame Romans into less self-destructive patterns of living. Gildas, a sixth-century British monk, wrote in utter anguish of the folly of his people which resulted in the invasion of Britain by the Germanic tribes. Although initially the Picts and Scots were a deadly scourge to the civilized Roman British populace, as far as Gildas was concerned, the Anglo-Saxons were worse. Gildas reports that Vortigern (whom he does not often mention by name, preferring the epithet 'tyrant') and the members of his council came up with a plan when they were faced by the hordes of barbarian Celts, namely, that they should invite Germanic mercenaries over to take on the job of defending their civilized country. According to Gildas, the first mercenaries took a liking to the land they had come to defend, and sent word home which brought more warriors from the continent. Then they picked quarrels with their hosts, and the stage was set for the Angles and Saxons to take by force what they wished from the British.

Gildas saw the Saxons as God's judgement on a whole range of sins which he denounced in the mode and the words of the biblical prophets. He was seldom explicit about what precisely was happening, and often enough self-contradictory. He saw the British as richly deserving of God's judgement for their vices, yet at the same time they were 'excellent hosts' to the Anglo-Saxons. A later Celtic writer, Nennius, gives an account, similar in substance to that of Gildas, of the events leading up to the Anglo-Saxon conquest, but with more detail. He tells us, for example, that Vortigern married the daughter of Hengest, one of the Saxon chiefs, but also had incestuous relations with his own daughter. These are vices at which the indignant but righteous Gildas only hints.

Tacitus wrote of men who were intensely competitive, of extravagant courage, eager for lavish reward, disposed to stand on their honour, and of the strictest sexual morality. Gildas's picture is not much different, except that instead of admiring these traits as manly virtues, he saw them as pagan savagery, mostly because he saw the practical results inflicted on his own people. Gildas had no admiration for the moral laxity of the British, but it was in some distant sense sanctioned by immemorial practice in Roman civilization. The virtues of the Germanic people were outlandish virtues, hard for the victims to appreciate.

# A CLASH OF CULTURES

Generally speaking, moral tracts and denunciations tend not to be the most historically balanced and reliable documents. In their different ways, both Tacitus's *Germania* and Gildas's *De Excidio Britanniae*, 'The Ruin of Britain', are moral tracts. Putting the evidence together is interesting in that it shows how different reactions to (broadly) the same cultural phenomenon can be. But looked at slightly differently, the texts give a clue to perhaps one of the root causes of the invasion.

The English conquest was part of the great movement of peoples, from about the time when Tacitus was writing in the first century, to about the time Gildas was writing in the sixth century. During this time, the Germanic tribes of northern, eastern and central Europe expanded and moved in all directions, conquering Rome and reducing the empire. But it is possible that the critical factor in the conquest of Britain may have been a clash of cultural values. The Britons wanted mercenaries, they got independent warriors with their own sophisticated ethical system. The Anglo-Saxon warriors demanded reward not pay, honour not just a living. They may well have despised the depraved behaviour of at least some of their 'excellent hosts', if Tacitus's description of the sexual ethics of the Germanic tribes has any basis in fifth-century reality, and if Nennius's description of British depravity is accurate. Finding themselves treated with indifference and contempt (Gildas uses that comprehensive and dismissive word *barbari*, 'barbarians'), the Germanic warriors could have decided to make their own fortunes in their own traditional way. This is, of course, only a possibility: we have to read between the lines.

It would be foolish to see the Anglo-Saxon conquest as a moral crusade. But it appears that the Christian Britons had accepted aspects of Roman culture that were quite possibly repugnant to heathen Germanic ethics as much as to Christian. Tacitus tried to correct the moral faults of the Romans by using the Germanic peoples as an example; Gildas saw these people as God's scourge. Perhaps the point is that Christian practice is never perfect, and there may be things to learn from the ethics of other cultures.

# THE HEROIC LIFE

Militarism was a condition of life in Anglo-Saxon England. Anglo-Saxon culture and history reflects at every turn the heritage of those early Germanic warriors who lived by predatory warfare. Conversion did not change this fact, though it mitigated the severity of institutionalized violence. Archaeological remains, especially grave goods, make this abundantly clear. Many pre-Christian males were buried with weapons and war-gear, spears, arrows, knives, swords, shields, mail-coats and helmets. The Anglo-Saxons had a keen eye for good weapons and a singular readiness to use them. The *Maxims* poet at one place expresses these sentiments:

> Glory goes with martial pride, bold men with the brave:
> both must be instantly ready for battle.
> The nobleman goes on horseback, the horse-troop rides in
> formation,
> the foot-soldiers stand firm.

Elsewhere, he notes that shields should be bound, covered with hide, swords decorated with gold, that bow and arrows should be a man's companions. He ends his poem on an ominous note:

> The shield must be ready, the javelin-head on the shaft,
> the edge sharp on the sword, the point on the spear,
> courage in fierce men, the helmet on the brave.
> And the cowardly will always get the least reward.

Most Anglo-Saxon men must have been familiar with the adrenaline rush of imminent battle. The different Anglo-Saxon kingdoms were frequently at war with each other, or with the Celts, or later with the vikings. The nobility practised the arts of war, honed their skills and developed an ethic centred around fighting. For them, it was proverbial that 'death is better than a life of shame', the shame attaching to anyone who ran away from battle, the shame of disloyalty. Throughout Anglo-Saxon times, the ordinary man could be called upon at any time to put his hand to the spear and turn out with his fellow labourers in the line of battle.

Apart from war, there was justice. Justice meant taking the law into your own hands, because nobody else would do it for you. If someone killed a member of your family, you would naturally try to kill one of theirs of approximately the same status. It was not merely revenge, but your bounden duty. Another proverbial expression was 'it is better for any man to avenge his friend than to mourn too much'. A constant preoccupation of the Anglo-Saxon kings was the loss of valuable men through blood feud. The kings in their law codes said that the offending party should pay a fixed sum of money for the person's life, called the *wergeld*, or a scale of penalties related to it for injury. But the fact that they kept on saying it in one law code after another suggests that not everyone took proper notice. King Alfred also made a law about people casually carrying spears around over their shoulders and accidentally gouging out eyes and laid down a penalty for that. Weapons were everywhere.

Perhaps the most striking thing about the instruments of war that have been recovered is the sheer elegance and lavish decoration of many of them. The Sutton Hoo sword, now in the British Museum, for example, was crafted from a number of steel rods of different levels of malleability, twisted together and hammered flat; then hard steel edges were welded to the central tongue. The finished blade has two qualities as a result:

it is flexible, and it has beautiful wavy patterns. This sword is by no means unique, and good blades were highly valued. Add to the Sutton Hoo blade a garnet-inlaid gold hilt and a richly embossed scabbard, and the weapon proclaims wealth, status and authority; but it is also utterly functional. And to emphasize that functionality, the curious article in the Sutton Hoo grave goods that has been called a sceptre is a carved piece of whetstone for honing blades. There are slim, delicately inlaid, silver-chased spear heads, some of them over two feet long, with the same kind of sinister beauty. People spent months or years working on these articles: lives and livelihoods alike depended on them.

## ASSIMILATION ...

The Germanic and heroic cast of vernacular literature and society is evident at every turn, and it points to some of the natural convergences of Christian and heroic which made conversion conceptually possible. It may seem strange that a society which had institutionalized warfare should have undergone a bloodless conversion. But it was so. In fact, it was relatively easy for those brought up with an ethic of loyalty to a human lord to understand and translate that loyalty into a spiritual principle. Loyalty to one's lord becomes loyalty to the Lord. Early missionaries went straight for the kings, knowing that if they could convert the kings, then the men would follow. In some cases this resulted in superficial conversions and later regression into heathen practices when kings reverted to heathenism. But loyalty to a secular lord, if he is a Christian, must mean that the one owing allegiance is also a Christian of some sort. Thus Christian teaching slips easily into a Germanic mould.

In a famous passage in the poetic saint's life *Andreas*, when St Andrew is about to set out on a sea journey to rescue St Matthew from cannibals in a foreign land, the ship owner (who is actually Jesus in disguise) suggests that Andrew's men stay on land and wait for him. They reply in words reminiscent of Peter's in John 6:69, 'Lord, to whom shall we go? You have the words of eternal life.' But the poem changes the details of the response, not only from the biblical one, but also from the Latin and Old English prose versions of the story:

> Where shall we turn, lordless,
> miserable, deprived of all that is good,
> wounded with sin, if we desert you?
> We would be hateful in every land,
> despised among the people, when the brave
> sons of men sit in counsel and discuss
> which of them best and unfailingly supported
> his lord in battle, when on the field of war
> in the malicious play of fight, hand and shield,
> eaten away by swords, endured hardship.

The Anglo-Saxon poet instinctively thought of loyalty as the bond of the warband, united in serving their lord, and of service as fighting. Here Andrew's men are closer to Germanic retainers than they are to Christian missionaries.

Just before his death in 709, Bishop Wilfrid of Ripon and York divided his treasure into the traditional Christian portions, for the poor, for the churches, for the clergy, and for churches to provide hospitality. But the clergy portion he allocates as a reward to the loyal clerics who had shared his exile; and he provides for rich gifts to buy the favour of secular rulers and bishops for his abbeys. He himself embraces the lord-retainer relationship towards his loyal companions, and he provides for a gift-exchange relationship between his abbeys and their secular and religious lords. Germanic cultural norms are naturalized in Christian culture.

Much later, in a battle against the vikings at Maldon in Essex, the Christian English general, Byrhtnoth, engages in very physical warfare to which he gives a spiritual slant (Text 14). He promises a messenger from the viking force who asks for money to buy them off, that they, the heathen, will die in battle. When he has been wounded by a viking in the attack which ensues, Byrhtnoth carefully spears him through the neck, laughs, and thanks God for the day's work. Dying, Byrhtnoth looks up to heaven, as Stephen the martyr did in the book of Acts, and prays to God to receive his soul. The Crusades, and the notion of holy war, are less than a century away at this point.

The Anglo-Saxons chose to focus on the pervasive military imagery in both Old and New Testaments and take it fairly literally. One of the dominant images of the Bible and the Middle Ages for the Christian is the *miles Christi*, the soldier of Christ: Erasmus's famous *Enchiridion Militis Christiani*, 'The Handbook of the Christian Soldier', was the culmination of a long line of works from Paul's second letter to Timothy, 'Endure hardship with us like a good soldier of Christ Jesus. No one serving as a soldier gets involved in civilian affairs' (2:3), which saw Christian faith as a kind of military service. The Christian must put on God's armour for the (spiritual) battle. We sense the parentheses around 'spiritual' in Anglo-Saxon attitudes, because everywhere there was fighting: some fought to live, others lived to fight.

Well-known in Anglo-Saxon England was the tradition of saints serving in armies in their youth: the great Gaulish St

Martin did, being 'accustomed to weapons from childhood' as Ælfric put it in his sermon on the life of the saint. St Oswald, king of Northumbria, who died in 641, was a soldier; St Guthlac, a notable saint of East Anglia, was also a military man in his youth. Bede's hero, the gentle and reclusive Cuthbert, had seen military service. And needless to say, the most Christian king of Anglo-Saxon England, King Alfred, spent the better part of his life fighting. None of this is surprising, since fighting was the expected duty of able-bodied, and especially well-born, men.

Of St Oswald and his battle against the usurpers of the Northumbrian throne, the gentle Anglo-Saxon scholar Ælfric wrote these very arresting words: 'Christ aided him in the slaying of his enemies'. Bede wrote a letter to Bishop Ecgberht of York to deplore the fact that monasteries (especially irregular ones) were, in the early eighth century, so common and so powerful that they engrossed the land that would otherwise have been given to pensioned-off warriors by the king (Text 15). Bede felt that monasteries were in this case undermining the social fabric by denying the rewards that were reasonably to be expected by heroes for their heroic labours.

## ... AND CONFRONTATION

Few Christian Anglo-Saxons would have equated fighting, especially against the heathen, with being unchristian; few Christian Victorians, frankly, would have had markedly different views on the matter. Christianity became the prevailing world view within the prevailing social conditions, and the resulting compromise was both strong and lasting. Superficial distinctions between 'heroic' and Christian, with the one proud, warlike and vengeful, the other humble, pacific and forgiving, are simplistic and misleading. As social and national policy, the Christian virtues hardly figured; just as they hardly figured in the Crusades, the Wars of Religion, the Reformation and after. Considerations of external security and social stability have consistently overridden Christian teaching in this matter from Anglo-Saxon times until now. Personal ethics and public policy were divorced soon after they were married, as Christianity took over the expansionism of the Roman Empire first, then fitted into the social system of the Germanic tribes.

But that is not to say that there was no attempt to modify the pre-Christian warband ethic. A counterpoint to the story of Byrhtnoth of Essex (Text 14) can be found in the story of King Edmund of East Anglia (Text 16). Edmund had the same 'request' for money from a viking force, and gave the same negative response. Inflamed with anger, the vikings march immediately on Edmund's hall, where they find him waiting. But instead of fighting, Edmund throws away his sword. He is captured, whipped and beaten, but enrages his captors further by constantly calling on the name of Jesus. Finally he is tied to a tree and made the target for spear and arrow, until (as Ælfric puts it in a moment of black humour) he is covered with the missiles like the bristles of a hedgehog. Both Byrhtnoth and Edmund were noblemen and both were revered after their deaths, though they expressed their faith in dramatically different ways.

An Anglo-Saxon cleric translated the last two-thirds of the book of Psalms into pretty ordinary Old English verse (Text 17). He might not have been a great poet, but he had a theological mind. In one of the most savage of the imprecatory Psalms, the original psalmist weeps by the rivers of Babylon, and proclaims of the one who gets revenge on the Babylonians, 'happy is he who repays you for what you have done to us

– he who seizes your infants and dashes them against the rocks'. The Anglo-Saxon 'translates' this as, 'happy is he who takes his own son and establishes him upon the Rock'. To the biblically educated reader or listener, the Rock would signify Christ, the cornerstone of the Church, or Peter the Rock, the spiritual head of the Church.

In preference to smashing children's heads, the translator urges people to establish their children in Christian truth, to build them on Christ and his Church. Thus the violence of even some parts of the Bible was modified and made more 'Christian', perhaps because the translator knew his audience's tendencies well enough to know they needed moderating. The great Bishop Ulfilas, missionary among the Gothic people in the first half of the fourth century, refused to translate the books of Kings from the Bible for the same reason – so as not to give encouragement to undesirable patterns of behaviour. And late in Anglo-Saxon England, Ælfric had serious hesitations about translating Genesis in case people started practising polygamy, incest and all the other not very Christian things that Genesis narrates (Text 18).

# INCULTURATION

Inculturation is the vogue word which was invented to express the kind of cultural interaction I have been describing. In Anglo-Saxon times it is where the spirit of Christianity is expressed in Germanic forms, from the most basic to the most sophisticated. In the language, Old English has 'three-ness' for Trinity, 'learning-youths' for disciples. In society, there is the Christian warrior, with his fierce loyalty to his Lord, who will fight to defend his home and family in service of his lord and his faith. There is also the Christian monk or saint, who will die for his Lord through the thousand-fold mortifications of the flesh, or face martyrdom in the cause of Christ. Age shall not weary them, any more than those who gave their lives self-sacrificially in later years, nor should the years condemn. Christianity is fully inculturated in Anglo-Saxon England.

Anglo-Saxon Christianity held up the highest standards of behaviour and commitment. Individuals strove to reach those standards, some in the heroic gesture, some in the dogged pursuit of daily holiness. But Anglo-Saxon Christianity is almost never individualistic: loyalties and obligations to Lord and lord, family, community, and fellow-Christians were an essential part of the enterprise of faith. The Anglo-Saxons would undoubtedly understand the value we place today on the individual, but they would not understand the emphasis in the Church and the world at large on individualism. The person who is focused solely on him or herself, in Anglo-Saxon England is either one of the holiest of people, the hermit doing spiritual battle against forces of evil – or the most miserable of people, an exile estranged from all that gives value and warmth to human life (Text 19).

# 4

## LIFE AND EXUBERANCE

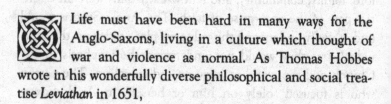Life must have been hard in many ways for the Anglo-Saxons, living in a culture which thought of war and violence as normal. As Thomas Hobbes wrote in his wonderfully diverse philosophical and social treatise *Leviathan* in 1651,

> Whatsoever ... is consequent of a time of Warre, where every man is Enemy to every man; the same is consequent to the time, wherein men live without other security, than what their own strength, and their own invention shall furnish them withall. In such condition, there is ... no account of Time; no Arts; no Letters; no Society; and which is worst of all, continuall feare, and danger of violent death; And the life of man, solitary, poore, nasty, brutish, and short. (Part I, Chapter 13)

This passage has been consistently quoted as characterizing the life of the Middle Ages in general. So it was for the Anglo-Saxons, and so it is for the many people in our modern world who have been victims and perpetrators of ethnic and tribal violence. But Christianity brought with it a great deal to liven and enlighten the world.

## THE APPEAL OF CHRISTIANITY

What, then, was the appeal of Christianity to people whose lives were nasty, brutish, and short; people who had institutionalized war and revenge; people who had pitifully inadequate resources against disease? The brief answer must be that Christianity offered all kinds of culture and literacy, an alternative ethic and authority for life, help for life's difficulties and hope for what was beyond. There was also a Christian counter-culture which rejected the prevailing social norm of war, and, by and large, practised the Christian virtues to a very marked degree: monasticism. In this chapter we will look at the kind of faith and practice the Anglo-Saxons developed, taking in monasticism, art and culture, biblical interpretation, and attitudes to issues of life.

## MONASTICISM

It was the monasteries which effected the conversion of Anglo-Saxon England. A good deal of missionary work in the north of England was carried out by the Irish missionaries sent from Iona, but based on Lindisfarne for the critical period from about 634 to the end of the eighth century, when the viking attacks began. From about AD 650, monasteries multiplied throughout the country: many disappeared later, and some we know of only from a single casual reference in a letter or other document. Some of the monasteries produced missionary bishops. Some, such as Breedon-on-the-Hill in Leicestershire, and Lindisfarne itself, became centres of bishoprics. They became centres of much more, taking the torch of classical and Christian learning from the Irish, and carrying it forward into the Middle Ages. But, at root, the monasteries gave meaning and reality to the Christian ideal of community.

The monasteries preserved, transmitted and produced literature and literacy, and this is perhaps what they are best remembered for. But they also combined the functions of hospital, hotel and orphanage with those of farm, cottage industry, trading centre, library, and occasionally, prison. Monasteries became major landowners. The monastic house pictured in Ælfric's *Colloquy* (a dialogue designed to help boys learn Latin, written at the end of the tenth century) has on the staff, as well as monks, ploughmen, shepherds, ox-herds, hunters, fishermen, fowlers, merchants, cobblers, salters, bakers, and last *and* least, a poor cook. Irish-influenced early monasticism put a great deal of emphasis on the solitary and self-denying life, but relatively quickly Anglo-Saxon monasteries adopted the Benedictine *Rule*, the most influential of all medieval guides to corporate monastic life, written by St Benedict of Nursia in Italy.

The *Rule* is a document which is both humane and deeply spiritual. It recognizes spiritual aspirations without ever forgetting that these aspirations dwell in fallible human beings. It provides for the highest attainment in spirituality through its focus on prayer and worship, while recognizing that for a community to be effective it needs discipline, regularity, work, learning, and most fundamentally, good human relationships. So the *Rule* sets out a pattern of service and offices throughout the day and night, but it adjusts them according to the seasons so that the monks do not get too tired. As well as providing for the spiritual growth of the monks through obedience and humility, it also makes sensible provision for the care of (for example) the monastery's gardening tools. Discipline of children, care of the elderly and sick, moderate and wise rebuke for those who fail to keep the standards of the house are all here. At the end of the *Rule*, Benedict makes clear that he has not said everything that could be said about holy living. But his *Rule* is designed to encourage monasteries in 'integrity of life'. This is precisely what it achieved.

The monasteries provided security in Anglo-Saxon England. Security within, where the *Rule* kept 'the unity of the Spirit in the bond of peace', and without, where the monasteries were a power for stability in the land. In Ireland, tribal warfare not infrequently targeted monasteries because they were viewed as the property of the clan. But in Anglo-Saxon England, not only were monasteries given charters which freed their lands and community from taxes and military service, they were held in such high regard they were effectively immune from attack until the viking raids. It was recognized that the monasteries were engaged in a different kind of warfare, against the world, the flesh and the devil.

Modern ideas of monasticism are conditioned to some extent by the Norman abbeys which remain. Even in their ruin, places like Fountains, Rievaulx and Whitby inspire awe, with their architecture drawing the eye and the mind together upwards. Dwarfed by the medieval abbey of Whitby, and lost under the detritus of centuries, lie the remains of the Anglo-Saxon monastery. This was one of the noblest houses of early Northumbria. Whitby was a 'double house', a monastery for both men and women, under the direction of Hild as abbess. The monastery was probably founded by Hild, the great-niece of King Edwin, with the encouragement of St Aidan, sometime around 650. The men and women were kept strictly segregated, and no whiff of scandal is ever attached to it in the sources. From what archaeologists can piece together, it seems that small wooden buildings, with some stone flooring and structural features, clustered inside a rampart. From the pattern of other sites it is possible to guess that the later Norman abbey obscures the larger communal buildings, probably stone-built. But even these would have none of the impressive proportions of the later abbey.

Few early Anglo-Saxon churches or monastic buildings exceed a hundred feet in length, few single chambers within those buildings exceed about sixty feet. Yet the remains from Whitby include coins and styli (writing implements), weaving, spinning and sewing implements, and some minor adornments. Put these alongside the literary record, with Bede telling us that in its early years it produced five bishops, as well as giving a home to Cædmon, the herdsman who became the first English Christian poet, and that in 664 it hosted a major royal council which decided the direction of Northumbrian Christianity – and together these sources give us a picture of a bustling community, more like a small town or indeed a university than a place of absolute spiritual seclusion.

One of the best short illustrations of the nature of Anglo-Saxon monasticism is found in a tenth-century Anglo-Saxon manuscript. This manuscript, now in St Petersburg, contains a Latin grammar. In a bit of spare space a scribe wrote, 'the learned smith must always work according to the pattern or exemplar, unless he is able to do better'. This implies that a monkish metalsmith might well be reading a Latin grammar in the monastic library, and be able to pick up a bit of snappy advice for his job as well as learning the finer points of Latin syntax or the ablative case. Learning and life in the smithy go together. It also shows how the past was valued, but not allowed to constrain: if the smith can do better than his pattern, more power to his elbow! Anglo-Saxon monasticism never lost touch with the real world. Through their books, the Anglo-Saxons show us how important learning was to them.

## CHRISTIAN ARTIFACTS

The founders of Anglo-Saxon monasticism were avid collectors of books particularly. Benedict Biscop, the founder of the great monasteries of Monkwearmouth and Jarrow, spent much of his life travelling in Europe to build up the libraries of his monasteries. He also imported paintings so that people who did not understand the services in church could look at the pictures and see episodes from sacred history. The vast explosion of writing that came with Christianity produced beautiful manuscripts and simple ones. Many have been lost, but are referred to in existing works. Some are exquisite in beauty, such as the *Codex Aureus*, the Golden Book, written on purple-stained vellum, in gold lettering, now kept in Stockholm; or the Lindisfarne Gospels now in the British Museum.

Some books are important for reasons other than their beauty, such as the stupendous *Codex Amiatinus*, a complete Bible copied in Northumbria less than a century after the first effective mission, which is an early witness for the text of the Bible in Latin. The word stupendous is no exaggeration. The book is so large and heavy it cannot be carried safely by one person; although it is austerely written and contains few illustrations, the quality of the script bears comparison with the Lindisfarne Gospels. Some books contain evidence of other kinds of importance. Several gospel-books have charters and manumissions (declarations of slave-freeing) written in spare space, suggesting that people saw these books as permanent, sacred, and above all, useful for recording the charitable acts of

Christian people. Certainly, the local farming industries, whether monastic or not, must have been stimulated by a demand for high-quality calf- or sheep-skin to be made into vellum: the *Codex Amiatinus* alone must have brought about the untimely death of at least five hundred calves, and probably many more.

# LITERATURE

Preserved in Anglo-Saxon manuscripts there are the standard works of theology, of biblical commentary and exegesis, the records of church councils, the lives of the saints, grammar, history, geography and science, service books and gospel books, penitentials and homilies, edifying and hortatory letters between scholars and bishops and missionaries and kings and monks and women religious. Nearly all these are in Latin. Latin is the language of the church and learning.

Let me give examples of the kind of Latin work we are dealing with, both from Alcuin. Alcuin lived from about 735 to 804, and was one of the most notable intellectuals of his day, moving from being head of the cathedral school at York to minister of education in France and Germany for Charlemagne. One of the most famous letters written in Anglo-Saxon England was Alcuin's to the bishop of Lindisfarne, Higbald (Text 20). Alcuin was in a situation where people had accepted Christianity in theory, but not yet let it influence them in practice. He heard that the brothers at Lindisfarne had actually been listening to heroic tales instead of the sermons of the Fathers, and his indignation could hardly be contained:

*Quid Hinieldus cum Christo?* What has Ingeld to do
with Christ? [he practically bawls at them] The house
is narrow, it cannot contain both. The king of the
heavens will have nothing to do with heathen and
damned so-called kings. For the eternal king rules in
the heavens, the lost heathen repines in hell.

What is usually seen as significant about this letter is that it
mentions a minor character in *Beowulf*, Ingeld, presumed to be
the hero of the kind of tales the brethren have been listening to.
And that it clearly outlines a not very liberal view on the salvation of those living before the preaching of the gospel, commonly held by churchmen of this age. Alcuin's attitude explains
at least in part the fact that we have almost no heathen literature from Anglo-Saxon England. It was simply not compatible
with Christianity. But while Alcuin is berating the brethren for
clinging to secular traditions, he is modelling to them the use
of Christian tradition, and expecting them to recognize it.

In the Bible, St Paul writes to the Corinthian church:

What do righteousness and wickedness have in common? Or what fellowship can light have with darkness?
What harmony is there between Christ and Belial?
What does a believer have in common with an un-
believer? (2 Corinthians 6:14)

Somewhat later, in the third century, the early church Father
Tertullian wrote,

What has Athens to do with Jerusalem? What has the
university to do with the Church? And what have
heretics to do with Christians?

And later still, in the fifth century, Jerome wrote,

> What has the Psalter to do with Horace, what have the
> gospels to do with Vergil, and St Paul with Cicero?

Through the Christian tradition, the problems of a mixed marriage or business partnership have become transmuted into a
concern for learning and literature, cleanly divided between
the heathen or heretical and the Christian. Alcuin is using
all the accumulated associations of Bible and Fathers to
persuade the monastery at Lindisfarne that secular song at
a monastic meal is a contradiction in terms. There is, then, a
kind of narrowness about Alcuin and Anglo-Saxon Christianity, but it is a narrowness which is self-defensive. Not only was
Alcuin aware of the secularity of the world around, he was also
aware of the advancing armies of the Moors in the south, and
the predatory ships of the vikings in the north. Only good doctrine and purity of life could offer hope in the gloom that was
closing in on the eighth-century Christian world.

   But there is also a cheerful and witty side to Alcuin, which
often escapes notice. John 21:11 tells us that when Jesus' disciples went fishing after the crucifixion they spent all night
fishing, but caught nothing. In the morning, Jesus appeared to
them on the shore and told them to throw the net over the
other side of the boat, and when they drew the net in 'it was
full of large fishes, 153, but even with so many the net was not
torn'. Now, Alcuin asks, what can be the significance of the
number 153, since meaning it must have? In various places, to
suit his message, he makes various suggestions (Text 21). This
is just one. He points out that the Ten Commandments signify
God's law for the world; add the seven gifts of the Holy Spirit
which signify the new dispensation in Christ, and the total is

seventeen. If you add up the numbers from one to seventeen, you get the total 153. If you split seventeen into ten and seven, seven divides again into three and four: three is the number of the Trinity, which represents the gospel of salvation, and four signifies the four corners of the world. So the incident in the gospel is 'really' telling us about the preaching of God's message to the world.

Alcuin is here drawing on a tradition of number symbolism which goes back to Judaism, and appears in most of the early church Fathers. It was regarded by Augustine of Hippo as fundamental to understanding the meaning of the Bible. 'Ignorance of numbers', he wrote in his important work *On Christian Doctrine*, 'prevents us from understanding things that are set down in Scripture in a figurative and mystical way.' Augustine himself goes on in his chapter to expound the passage in John in a slightly different way from Alcuin, but using the same methods.

Modern scholars have made heavy weather of this kind of interpretation. *The Cambridge History of the Bible* suggests that 'most readers will recoil before an exegetical ingenuity so subtle and fecund and, withal, so laboured and unconvincing'. It is true that by this method, spiritual lessons might be drawn from a shopping list as readily as the Bible. But two points should be noted. Firstly, the interpretation reached by number symbolism ties in absolutely with the biblical context, where the incident leads to the commissioning of the disciples to preach to all the world. And secondly, it ties in with a different way of looking at things which is entirely in tune with the quirkiness that we find elsewhere in Old English literature. This play with numbers is like Alcuin's play with words when he writes whole paragraphs in words beginning only with the letter 'p'. It shows an ability to see things from the underside, a playful juggling with concepts, a narrow dividing line between serious and silly. And an intellectual joy and relish in tradition and its ability to expand beyond its original confines.

## A BIG BOOK AT EXETER

If Alcuin's orthodoxy has a certain narrowness, we learn something from his letter to Lindisfarne about the breadth of Anglo-Saxon monasticism. Monks listened to heroic, presumably secular tales, and no doubt enjoyed them. The larger part of the Anglo-Saxon contribution to world civilization was in preserving both Christian and secular classics. Books were produced in monasteries, except for a few, mainly functional and rather dull works, which were written for kings. But the vernacular works – poems particularly, which are both Christian and composed in the Germanic language and style of the ordinary Anglo-Saxons – are worthy of attention, not least because they are less bound by the need for orthodoxy. Not only is there *Beowulf*, which offers a challenge to the prevailing theological understanding, as exemplified by Alcuin, of the fate of the unconverted heathen. There are also vernacular poems which confound all modern expectations of monastic production. The Exeter Book is a book which shows the breadth of Anglo-Saxon Christianity very clearly.

The Exeter Book is a largish book of poetry in Old English. It is thought to be the book referred to as 'one large English book of miscellaneous pieces in poetry' in the list of the donations of Bishop Leofric of Exeter to his cathedral library in 1072. At any rate, there does not seem to be any other volume that quite fits the description. It is very much a miscellany, with major poems on religious themes. There is the liturgical poem *Christ*, a delightful Old English version of the Advent antiphons now best known through J. M. Neale's 'O come, O come Emmanuel'. There are two poems joined together about an East Anglian saint, *Guthlac*, and another on a female Roman saint, *Juliana*; there is the biblical poem *Azarias* (otherwise known as 'The Song of the Three Children'), the allegorical poem *The Phoenix*, various homiletic poems like *The Judgment Day*, *Alms-Giving*. And a dialogue between the soul and the body where the soul reproaches the body for its indulgence which has led to the soul being damned – this poem enterprisingly entitled *Soul and Body* by modern editors. These are the kinds of poems we would expect in a book produced in a monastery.

But alongside these are two poems preserving ancient Germanic traditions, *Widsith* and *Deor*, and three poems (or a poem in three parts) preserving popular wisdom, *Maxims*. Two further poems give voice to laments from women. And the Exeter Book preserves a collection of riddles, without which we would hardly know that this genre of literature existed in Old English. This in itself argues for wide cultural tastes, and a liberal and open attitude to literature from various sources. When we look more deeply at the women's poems and the riddles, we see a Christianity able to cope with the dissonance and distress of life, and able to find humour in some of it.

## MARGINAL WOMEN?

Women tend to figure only marginally in the major heroic dramas of Old English. There is an exception to this pattern which is worth noticing: there are as many lives of female saints in Old English verse as there are male. Figuring marginally in heroic dramas does not of course mean women were marginalized. Before the Norman Conquest women had probably as much self-determination as they did early in the twentieth century. They could inherit and dispose of property, they could rule large communities, they could marry and divorce according to their choice for the most part. And there were heavy legal penalties for rape, abduction, injury and insult against women. The Norman Conquest brought about a very significant deterioration in the status of women, and this was anticipated in some ways by ecclesiastical law. In later Old English versions of Frankish-influenced penitentials, some penalties for sexual indiscretion, polyandry, for example, involve execution for the woman; whereas a man may keep a wife and concubine (or several) with only the strong disapproval of the Church.

## WOMEN IN THE LYRICAL ELEGIES (TEXTS 22 AND 23)

The Exeter Book contains a number of poems that have been called elegies. They are basically Christian, homiletic pieces reflecting on experiences of exile enforced and chosen, and drawing consolation from the prospect of 'mercy from the Father in heaven, where for us all security remains'. The poems focus on the decay of all worldly life and wealth, the insecurity of human relationships. The interesting thing is that the same kind of experience for a female character in a poem called *The Wife's Lament* gives rise to no homiletic reflection and no vision of Christian security. Another poem about a woman's experience, *Wulf and Eadwacer*, has the same elegiac features. But like *The Wife's Lament*, it has no mention of God, and draws no Christian lessons. There is a distinct lack of consolation for misery in these two women's poems, and it leaves the reader uncertain and uneasy.

# EMOTIONS

The language of *The Wife's Lament* and *Wulf and Eadwacer* is desperately ambiguous. *Wulf* in particular has been interpreted by several scholars as a riddle because of the uncertainty of the storyline and the relations between the characters. Not one person is named in *The Wife's Lament*. The names of *Wulf* and *Eadwacer* only add to the ambiguity, since Wulf, for example, could be a shortened form of dozens of names, as well as the name of the animal. What is not uncertain in these poems, however, is the depth of feeling. The woman in *Wulf and Eadwacer* laments that Wulf is separated from her on an island in the fens, and she cries in the rain. The woman in *The Wife's Lament* regrets that she has no friends among her lord's people, and once he has gone they start picking on her and plotting against her. She has to live in a dreary cave in a dark and miserable grove, and each day starts wearily at dawn and drags on forever as she sits alone under an oak tree crying.

*Wulf and Eadwacer* seems to be about a love-triangle, where the woman is attached to one man and married to another. It ends with the telling sentiment,

> It is easy to wrench apart what was never joined –
> our song together.

The word for song, *giedd*, can mean other things. The image is a powerful one. Love is a song, a story, a jest, a riddle. But here it is a song without harmony, a story without a happy ending, a jest without a punchline, a riddle without a solution. An essential part is missing, because the parts were never properly joined. There is probably an echo of Jesus' words in Matthew 19:6, 'what God has joined together, let man not separate', acknowledging that God never put the two lovers together. And to make the point yet more striking, the final line is short, lacking a whole half-line.

*The Wife's Lament* is just as plangent. She is married to a man who has to go away and leave her with his family. She is so miserable that she tries to follow, but is eventually forced to live alone in a desolate place. Her husband turns against her and she finds deadly deception in the man who formerly had promised so much:

> Very often we promised
> that nothing but death, and death alone,
> should separate us. That is changed;
> our love is now as if
> it had never been.

There is the smell of death over the poem: the woman is forced to live in an earth-cave in a grove; the word for 'earth-cave' is used elsewhere of the grave or tomb, and the murder contemplated by the man might be the murder of their relationship. Their love and the vows they made 'till death us do part', are now things of the past. And the woman sums it all up at the end with a proverbial maxim:

> Woe from longing is the lot
> of the one who has to wait for a loved one!

This expression of woe is used elsewhere throughout Old English literature, poetry and prose, to express the horrors of hell. Like Mephistopheles in *Doctor Faustus*, the woman says in her suffering, 'this is hell, nor am I out of it ... Where we are is hell'.

Scholars have put a particular spin on the gendered language of *The Wife's Lament* recently. The Church or the soul, both feminine in Old English, could be represented by the abandoned woman of *The Wife's Lament*. With a bit of imagination, the details of the elegy could fit into this, while making sense on their own. The last lines, 'Woe it is', would then be a climactic statement about how the Church or the soul lives on in its earth-cave (in the body, perhaps, or on earth), experiencing the hell of being without Christ its lover, and awaiting his coming with longing. All this kind of imagery was popular in the early medieval church.

Situations and people far from ideal figure here. *Wulf and Eadwacer* and *The Wife's Lament* are about situations that are real and difficult, about vital emotions and relationships, about mess and love, longing and regret. We respond not only to the suffering person, but see in her some of the difficulties and tragedies we all face. These women's elegies in particular enable us to appreciate the desperation and misery of people driven by conventional expectations into untenable situations. They raise theological questions by their very being.

Though neither *Wulf and Eadwacer* nor *The Wife's Lament* mentions God or any aspect of religion directly, they were written by a scribe, if not by poets, whose world view was Christian. There are echoes of Christian concepts in them, hints that help us interpret the poems. The monk who compiled the Exeter Book did not shy away from poems which did not fit into the mould of Christian consolation. The poems look with steady, but unjudging eyes at the miseries women experience. The experience of women challenges the reader, as the experience of Job, the great poet of despair, does in the Bible. There are no easy answers. This book does not marginalize women, but gives space to their particular difficulties. It speaks of a Christianity which respects people, feels with them, and does not easily judge or condemn. Women were important in Anglo-Saxon Christianity. It gave a voice to the powerless, appealing to those who were suffering.

## 'IT IS THE GLORY OF GOD TO CONCEAL A MATTER ...'

No part of life is missing from the Exeter Book and Anglo-Saxon Christianity: they are all-embracing. And a robust sense of humour is evident in a number of short poems in the collection. Perhaps the most arresting feature of the Exeter Book is the fact that it includes nearly all the Anglo-Saxon riddles that are known. These are the most exuberant poems we have in Old English. Riddles were popular among the Germanic peoples, as we know from the riddle games of Old Norse literature. Latin riddles were composed in the fourth or fifth century by a writer called Symphosius, about whom little is known. But a number of leading Anglo-Saxon clerics wrote riddles in Latin too. Aldhelm, bishop of Sherborne, Tatwine, archbishop of Canterbury, and Eusebius *alias* Hwætberht, abbot of Monkwearmouth, all contemporaries of Bede, composed riddles, some of which are translated in the Exeter collection.

What is interesting about the Exeter group is the range of subjects and types. The closest parallel to the riddle in the modern world is the crossword: so in the riddles there are word puzzles, ambiguity, acrostics, allusions to literature, all sorts of misleading and cryptic references, just like the modern crossword. Among them is one fairly typically describing a creature with one eye, two ears, two feet, 1200 heads, a back, a front, two arms, one neck and two sides. The poet closes the riddle, characteristically, with 'say what I am called', and of course

everyone will instantly reply, 'a one-eyed garlic seller'! This is
a genuine riddle. The so-called 'book-moth riddle' is actually
borrowed from Symphosius, and is more of a *jeu d'esprit* than
a riddle, a playful, punning and witty little piece which gives
away the solution in the first word. Another riddle begins with
the Old English equivalent of 'My name is *wob* (anag.)', where
the solution is 'bow'. There are riddles with the solution in
runes, and some where we do not know the solutions, the
ambiguity or obscurity is so effective. Some are secular, dealing
with weapons or drinking horns, others are religious, including
several on the cross and gospel-books.

One riddle crosses the boundaries we might want to draw,
being a genuine enigma, religious in reference, but touching
on the taboo subject of incest.

> A man sat at wine, with his two wives,
> and his two sons, and his two daughters,
> dear sisters to each other, and *their* two sons,
> noble firstborn sons. The father of each of
> those princes was in there with them,
> uncle and nephew together. In all there were five
> noble men and noble women sitting there.

It deals with the Bible story of Lot's daughters from Genesis,
and only those who know the biblical source will be able to
guess the riddle. Fearing that they would not be able to
marry and have children, Lot's daughters got their father
drunk, slept with him, and both had sons. There were five of
them in Lot's family, then, but the riddle explores nearly all
the possible relationships between them to give the impression
there were more. If you did not understand before why Ælfric
was hesitant about translating the Old Testament for the

ordinary reader, now you might see it better.

The humour of this riddle is delicate. A man drinking with his family around him is a picture of intimacy and normality. But when we realize that Lot was drunk when he was taken advantage of and fell into the sin of incest, the drinking of wine takes on a barbed irony. And the language of nobility used of the family members increases the closer we get to realizing that all of them were implicated in the most fearful of sins. Finally, one of the most important and closest of relationships among the Germanic peoples, the sister's son, uncle-nephew relationship, is here too close, since the uncle is also the father. The poet uses the Bible narrative and the riddle format to draw the sting of a taboo subject. He allows people to laugh at something which is very serious indeed, without diminishing its seriousness.

There is one type of riddle that is not included in most collections. The deliberately bawdy sexual innuendo of several riddles is hard to reconcile with the sober religious matter of the rest of the book (Text 24). There are plenty of popular riddles relating especially to the male appendage – for one in the Exeter collection, the solution is 'poker'. In the light of what we have said about women, it is significant that the butt of the joke in most of these riddles is male. They are not obscene because they do not make people the objects of lust; they are bawdy in finding humour in sexual innuendo.

But the interesting question is how to fit these into the monastic context. The best explanation I have heard is the 'purity game', where monks sit round and tell riddles, and the first one to snigger is 'out'. By bringing sex into the open, in a witty, joking way, its disruptive power for celibate monks is diminished. Whatever the real explanation, these poems have a liveliness and vigour, a bawdy earthiness and sharpness of observation, a relish in words and things that we would not otherwise know about. I wonder whether Bishop Leofric had read his big book of miscellaneous pieces in Old English verse. I like to imagine he had, and that he had a quiet chuckle or two over it.

## RELISH FOR LIFE

The contribution of the monasteries to Anglo-Saxon Christianity was very great. But just as the modern idea of a monastery as a place of seclusion has to be adjusted in the face of the evidence from Anglo-Saxon England, so also modern ideas of humourless and spiritually introverted monks and nuns have to be adjusted in the light of the literary productions of Anglo-Saxon monastics. The Benedictine *Rule* counselled against too ready laughter. But there is a delight in words and ideas in Anglo-Saxon England, and a willingness to face life's difficulties and threats with courage and humour that has a timeless appeal. Anglo-Saxon Christianity was a religion that loved life and learning. The Anglo-Saxons cultivated an attitude towards tradition that drew out the important things from it. But they did not allow tradition to stifle their response to the troubling and absurd, nor did they exclude these things from their understanding of faith.

Anglo-Saxon Christianity, like that of some later eras, used language with delight and sensitivity, with a creativity that was mirrored in other arts like book production and illumination. Modern Christianity has tended to wed itself to a bland scientism which is suspicious of art and any feeling or emotion other than generalized happiness. Or it has married itself to tradition, which only allows experience to speak in language and music centuries old. Childishness and irrelevance are often the results. The Christian smith of Anglo-Saxon times bashed out his faith on the anvil, the scholar crafted his words from tradition into life, the poet took in what was around him or her in order to speak to the heart and the mind. Anglo-Saxon Christianity has exuberance and life.

# 5

# CHRISTIANITY: CELTIC OR ROMAN?

 One of the central issues facing Anglo-Saxon Christianity was the question of authority. In the north, the Celtic missionaries had been effective in converting kings and people. In the south, the Roman mission had been just as effective. But there were differences between the two types. Celtic Christianity, practised by British and Irish Christians alike, was a vigorous local offshoot from the main root of Christianity in the west. It had developed its own style, and independent traditions. Roman Christianity had also developed since the planting of Christianity in Celtic lands, and the two diverged on a number of points of practice. Anglo-Saxon Christianity was caught between the two.

Ireland had never been a Roman province, and the Irish church had always been at the edges of Roman Christianity, a barbarian church of limited interest to the Popes. As a result some aspects of developing catholicity had passed the Irish by. In Bede's time, the Celtic church and the Roman church were incompatible in one major area: the dating of Easter. Easter is a 'moveable feast', and does not have a fixed date, but is calculated in relation to the phases of the moon. In some years, the Celtic church celebrated Easter a week before the Roman church. Other less important areas of difference related to the working out of the Christian life. For example, Celtic Christianity was fundamentally monastic, and bishops did not have dioceses as such, but were subject to the abbot of the monastery where they were based.

Northumbria owed much to the Irish, but after the initial conversion the church in Northumbria looked beyond Ireland for its development and growth. In particular, the founder of Bede's monasteries of Monkwearmouth and Jarrow, the Northumbrian nobleman Benedict Biscop, spent much of his life and wealth journeying to Rome for books and relics and craftsmen to enrich Northumbrian monasteries. Rome's influence soon overshadowed the Celtic. Bishop Wilfrid had disputes with successive kings and archbishops, and in his difficulties, it was to Rome and the Popes that he made his appeal. The Popes had far more influence than any Irish abbot.

Choices can be difficult. At some point the Anglo-Saxon church had to choose between the two main influences upon it. And this choice between Celtic and Roman was a particularly painful one. The writings of the Venerable Bede, who lived from 673 to 735, perhaps the most painful period of adjustment, touch again and again on the issue. Bede was all for the Roman pattern of Christianity, but his honesty consistently prevents him from allowing his preference to become prejudice. We see in his writings an awareness of what the church was losing as well as what it was gaining in having to make the choice. In this chapter we will look at how the decision was reached, and what factors had influence in the decision. And we will consider Bede's character and writings to see whether he was unduly obsessive about this matter.

# CONFRONTATION

Bede tells how St Augustine of Canterbury tried to co-operate with the British church in evangelizing the heathen English (Text 10). He also tried to bring them into line over the dating of Easter. He held two conferences with the British bishops to try and hammer out an agreement. In the first, discussions failed because the British bishops 'preferred their own traditions to those which the church throughout the world accepts in Christ'. In desperation Augustine tried to convince them by means of a miracle contest. He healed a blind man when the British bishops could not, but they nevertheless would not abandon their customs without the consent of their people.

Before the second conference, the British bishops consulted a hermit over the issue. The advice was that they should arrange their own test. Augustine was to arrive at the conference before the British. The test was that if he rose to his feet as a sign of respect when the British bishops came in, then he was 'meek and lowly of heart', and should be listened to. Augustine did not rise, and the British bishops did not agree to his proposals. As a result (as Bede records it), a decade later the heathen king of Bernicia, Æthelfrith, ravaged British lands. The horrors culminated in the Battle of Chester some time before 616, when Æthelfrith massacred twelve hundred unarmed monks from the monastery of Bangor, who had gathered to pray for a British victory in the battle (Text 25).

Bede tells this story in a frankly partisan fashion. He is never in any doubt that the British bishops were wrong. Having been hounded and harried to the outer edges of the land they once occupied, the British were understandably reluctant to bring any benefit, let alone the benefit of salvation, to their persecutors. But to refuse to acknowledge the authority of the universal church, and the miracle performed through Augustine in confirmation of his authority, Bede saw as blameworthy. The British had elevated their own traditions to a place of absolute authority, and insisted on an inappropriate humility in Augustine. So they were punished as heretics.

There does not seem to be any great logic here. Roman traditions were as much tradition as British ones. Augustine's miracle competition was as much a test as the British humility test was. Argument had failed and caprice took over. Though Bede tries hard, he does not manage to portray this sorry interlude as creditable on either side. The British proudly insisted on humility, the Romans threatened impotently. The scene was set for more acrimony at a later date.

## ST CUTHBERT

Bede spent a great deal of time arguing and writing about the correct way of dating Easter, perhaps the most important of the issues at stake. The precise details are of little interest now, and that is perhaps testimony to the effectiveness of Bede's campaign. He was sometimes immoderate in his comments on the British and their adherence to the Celtic pattern. But he had a great admiration for the Irish Celtic Christians who were also wrong in this respect as far as he was concerned. His great hero was St Cuthbert. Cuthbert was a product of the Irish monastic system, and his virtues as saint, bishop and hermit were the Celtic virtues of asceticism, punishing the body as a hindrance to the soul.

Bede wrote two *Lives* of the saint, one in verse and one in prose. Both rely for their information on the earlier *Life* by an anonymous writer of Lindisfarne. The anonymous *Life* of Cuthbert was written in the last years of the seventh century.

Bede claimed in the traditional way to be improving the style of his original, but actually he edited the material carefully where it suited him.

In one of the loveliest stories related of Cuthbert, he is portrayed as immersing himself in the cold sea, an Irish penitential practice to combat lust (Text 26). When he emerges from the sea, two otters come and rub themselves against him to dry him, and breathe on him to warm him up. The animal story type is one which is distinctively Celtic, and there are small indications that Bede was uneasy with animal stories of this kind. Nevertheless, Bede related the story, with only slight changes from the Lindisfarne original. So Bede respected not only Cuthbert's saintliness, but also the integrity of the story in which it was displayed – even though the story was not quite to his taste.

Bede could not resist the temptation to improve on his original when it came to the saint's death-bed speech, however (Text 27). The speech and attitude of the dying saint is given great prominence in hagiography, because it is the most profound statement of the saint's claim to sanctity. And at the same time, it is the saint's last opportunity to edify the audience: 'famous last words'. When Bede himself was dying, a disciple was on hand diligently to record every last word. The anonymous writer was content to record only Cuthbert's saintly gestures of raising eyes and hands to heaven, and the commending of his soul to God. Bede managed to slip in a warning against the 'schismatics' who persisted in the Celtic observance of Easter, and had Cuthbert urge his listeners to avoid all contact with such. This is pure Bede, not at all the historical Cuthbert.

# ST AIDAN

St Aidan was another wholly admirable Celtic Christian written about by Bede (Text 28) – except of course in his adherence to the Celtic Easter. In a painfully honest chapter Bede discusses his significance: the first bishop of Lindisfarne, friend and counsellor of King Oswald, and the gentle evangelist of Northumbria. Bede is full of admiration for his character, his faithfulness and his effectiveness. But he is sorely troubled by Aidan's 'unorthodoxy', and he struggles to accommodate the facts he knows of Aidan's deep spiritual power, with his awareness that his practice was schismatic. He ties himself up in knots in a way that is as commendable as it is amusing. Bede was not insensitive to paradox, and was not entirely without the ability to face up to the inconsistencies of his own assumptions.

There is a good deal more to this issue than prejudice or xenophobia. Bede loved and admired the Celtic missionaries who had brought the gospel to the bloodthirsty Germanic tribes of the north of England. He loved and admired their rigour and selflessness, their utter commitment, their learning, their gentleness combined with spiritual strength. Yet so great was his enthusiasm for the Roman cause that he saw them as a threat to true Christianity. It is clear to us that his age got the issue out of proportion. The heat generated was neither felt nor appreciated by later generations, as will be the case with most of today's topical debates. But some reflection on the detail and meaning of this issue is important for our understanding of Anglo-Saxon Christianity.

# WHITBY, 664 (TEXT 29)

As far as Bede was concerned, the fundamental issues of dispute between the Irish and the Roman church were settled for good and all by the Council of Whitby in 664. The need for some decision on the correct way to calculate Easter had become apparent to King Oswiu of Northumbria because one year he observed the Celtic practice and celebrated Easter a week earlier than his wife Eanflæd, who had been brought up in Kent, an area evangelized by Augustine's Roman mission. He called a council at Abbess Hild's monastery of Whitby, where the issues could be debated and resolved. The main speakers were Bishop Colman of Lindisfarne on the Celtic side, and Wilfrid on the Roman side.

In Bede's account, when Colman outlines the Celtic position in relation to Easter, he is devastatingly rebutted by Wilfrid on all counts. Towards the close, the debate boils down to the fact that Colman relies on the authority of perhaps the greatest and most respected of Irish saints after Patrick, Columba. Against him, Wilfrid pits the authority of St Peter. The comparison does Columba no favours and he is dismissed, almost contemptuously, as 'your Columba'. All agreed to adopt the Roman custom, concludes Bede. But preferring to keep the customs of his forefathers, Colman left the council, and later Northumbria, with those of a like mind. Bede briefly records that Colman set up a monastery in Mayo, Ireland, which experienced all sorts of troubles until it embraced the catholic Roman discipline.

Bede gives us the only record we have of the detail of the discussion, and it is perhaps his imagination which controls the presentation of the argument. It is not surprising, then, that the Roman side has the best lines. But it is worth noticing that resort is made to that feeblest of arguments, 'our saint is better than your saint', and that Bede overcomes his dislike of Wilfrid in giving him the stronger logic. On the principle that the more indifferent a case is, the better the presentation it requires, it might be reasonable to deduce that the debate was more evenly balanced than Bede was prepared to admit. It is highly probable that the enforcement of the council's decision was more painful than Bede acknowledges. Monasteries -- Lindisfarne certainly, and Hexham probably -- were taken over from their Celtic observances and put into the hands of Roman abbots. In this narrative, as in others, Bede portrays the issues in black and white, when the modern reader might see a spectrum of greys.

Hindsight is useful in this instance. It allows us to step back from the debate and consider wider questions. With the benefit of hindsight, it is possible to say that the decision of Whitby was one which brought benefit to both Anglo-Saxon and Celtic Christianity, because this decision had a major influence on the Celtic church entering into catholic unity with the whole western church. Yet neither Celtic nor Anglo-Saxon Christianity lost their distinctive nature through the change. In fact, both grew into more flexible ethnic Christian communities.

## CELTIC OR ROMAN?

The Irish Celtic church that had so much influence in Northumbria was unquestionably an effective missionary organization. Their monasteries provided intellectual and spiritual bases for the enterprise, and supporting teams of workers and encouragers. Celtic Christianity depended, nevertheless, on a radical separation between secular and religious life. English

Christianity by the time of Bede had expanded beyond the confines of the monastery, and involved kings and politics, territories and estates, power and influence. The concern for Anglo-Saxon Christianity was not so much separation of secular and religious but of integration. The question was not so much how to convert people, but how to manage the church in England. The conversion was largely if superficially complete. The difficulty was to help people to live in a Christian fashion, to mould society to reflect Christian moral ideals. English Christianity was effectively facing similar problems and opportunities to those faced by the Roman church at the time of the Roman emperor Constantine, namely how to emerge from a tightly knit missionary bud into a full-blown state religion. It is hardly surprising that it should look to Rome for a lead in this.

Monasticism was not abandoned by the Anglo-Saxon church in this early period about which Bede wrote. For the Anglo-Saxons, monasticism remained the Christian counter-culture, just as it did in the Celtic church. But it was important that monasteries, though free of secular taxes and dues, should be under the authority of properly consecrated bishops. Roman bishops had a territorial remit like Roman imperial governors before them. Celtic ones had honour but not authority in this respect. Bede recommended that Bishop Ecgberht should put down false monasteries in his diocese: bishops under the authority of an abbot after the Celtic manner did not have such matters in their jurisdiction.

We have already seen that the Benedictine *Rule* was as humane as it was spiritual. Celtic monasteries had a bewildering variety of monastic Rules, some more humane than others. But extreme self-denial and the solitary life of the hermit remained the ideals of Celtic Christianity. St Cuthbert fled from his episcopal responsibilities to his hermitage on the

Farne Islands, and practised the penitential discipline of immersing himself in the cold sea. Both of these were Celtic practices, and were essentially personal and private, though of course they had public implications. At its most extreme, Celtic Christianity was dualistic: it held the body to be evil and the spirit to be good. Roman ideals were more communal, and in a different way no less difficult to attain. Discipline was a means to an end, the better service of God and the community. Not only was this more moderate in terms of its understanding of the relation of body and spirit, but it also fitted better with Anglo-Saxon social organization. Once again, for a variety of reasons, the Anglo-Saxon church leaned towards a Roman type of theology and practice.

There was a great deal at stake at Whitby. Adopting Roman Christianity would bring the English church into the mainstream of Christendom. It would conform to the norms and ideals of the apostles, saints and Fathers of the universal church. Adopting Celtic Christianity would put the English church at the edge of civilization, adhering to antiquated and inadequate doctrines and practices no longer sanctioned by the universal Body of Christ. So it was almost inevitable that the Anglo-Saxon church should choose Roman Christianity. The fact that within a hundred years the Roman rite had been adopted throughout Ireland and the Celtic realms is testimony to the power of the ideas as much as the power of the kings, bishops and nobles who first embraced them.

## AN ILLUSTRATION FROM LINDISFARNE

The Lindisfarne Gospels might help us better to understand the situation of the Anglo-Saxon church. Many people are familiar with the glorious illuminations and the sumptuous colour of the carpet pages. The designs of the book are endlessly intricate, with geometrical interlace and animal ornament twisting around a central motif, often the cross. The book was made probably at the extreme end of the seventh century at Lindisfarne. We know quite a bit about it, because it was annotated by a monk called Aldred about the middle of the tenth century. He tells us Bishop Eadfrith of Lindisfarne wrote the book, Bishop Ethelwald made the cover and bound it, and Billfrith the hermit decorated the cover with gold, silver and precious stones.

The designs in the book combine Celtic and Germanic styles. The Lindisfarne library must have had books from Ireland as well as from Italy and other parts of Europe. The so-called Incarnation initial of Matthew's gospel, the great Greek letter *chi* with its X-shape sweeping out to the four corners of the page, has enclosed decorated circles around its edges. These are very similar to those on a famous Irish cloak pin, the great Tara Brooch. Many other similarities with Irish art have been noticed. The display script on the capital pages, in square and rounded capital letters, has features in common with those in Irish and Welsh manuscripts. The base script of the book is called 'half-uncial' and it is the script the Anglo-Saxons learned from the Irish missionaries. Without question, the Lindisfarne book owes a great deal to Irish inspiration.

The book is written in Latin, of course. The Irish were great scholars and used that language with fluency. The missionaries, in particular, knew their Latin scriptures. They passed on to the Anglo-Saxons knowledge of the language the scriptures were available in, and an art which matched in its subtlety and beauty that of the book's message. And what did Aldred do with this book which was already two hundred and

fifty years old when it fell into his hands? He wrote all over it
in his sprawling Anglo-Saxon 'minuscule' script. And he wrote
in his own dialect of Anglo-Saxon, not even the standard
dialect of the court. Surely this is an outrageous example of
vandalism!

It is, if the value of a book lies only in its art. But gospel-
books, as we noticed earlier, are important for much more. If we
were so inclined, we could see Aldred's translation of the text
and his explanatory notes as adding to the value of the book.
Certainly, Aldred's purpose was to make the book intelligible to
his contemporaries. And his marginal comments show that he
assumed very little about the level of education of those who
were reading the book. In Aldred's day, people could read, but
not much in Latin. And what they could read in Old English,
they could not necessarily understand. So, next to Matthew
1:18, '[Jesus'] mother Mary was pledged to be married to
Joseph', Aldred comments, 'to take care of [her], not at all to
have as a wife'. Next to John 1:1, 'In the beginning was the
Word, and the Word was with God', Aldred notes, 'In the
beginning was the Word: that is, God's Son, [and the] Word
was with God the Father'. Aldred wanted to be sure that people
understood the theology of what they were reading.

This is another example of Anglo-Saxon Christian pragmatism. It was more important that people should understand
the gospels than that they should marvel at the art-work.
Celtic Christianity had given the Anglo-Saxons an intelligible
gospel and beautiful art. But the needs of the Anglo-Saxon
church were different from those of the Celtic missionaries,
and indeed the Celtic church as a whole. Learning was in
decline, and even the style of handwriting had changed. For
books to be useful, they needed to be understood. And for the
church to have influence, it had to meet the needs of ordinary

people. There is pain in leaving behind things of beauty, and examples of courage and grace. But Anglo-Saxon Christianity grasped the fact that the Christian life is lived in the present, in obedience to God, and in response to the prompting of circumstances.

There was a hard edge of pragmatism about the decision of the Council of Whitby. The notion that there might be varieties of interpretation, or matters of peripheral significance, or traditions which are equally valid in the long view, is one foreign to the world view of the whole of medieval Christianity. And consequently the perfectly harmless variations practised by the Celtic church were seen by Bede and others as dangerous to the whole enterprise. So there had to be a choice. Something was lost in leaving behind Celtic Christianity. But Roman practices and unity with the wider church of Europe was what Anglo-Saxon Christianity needed.

## BEDE

We have taken the liberty of disagreeing with Bede's evaluation of the importance of the issue of the dating of Easter and the choice between Roman and Celtic. This is difficult in that Bede's record of the Council of Whitby is the only one we have. It raises a different issue, and that relates to Bede's motivation. If he was obsessive about the dating of Easter, and that was not as important as he thought, can we trust his judgement on other matters? Does he have feet of clay? What, in fact, do we know about him? If we can understand Bede, then we have a reasonable chance of understanding Anglo-Saxon Christianity and its perspective on these matters.

Bede is arguably the most important early English historian. Virtually nothing is known about him that he does not tell us himself or reveal through his works (Text 30). We have to guess from his words when he was born, and it seems to have been 672 or 673. At the age of seven he was handed over by his family to Abbot Benedict Biscop, founder of the monasteries of Monkwearmouth and Jarrow, for education. We do not know the circumstances of this transaction. Bede might have been an oblate, a kind of donation by pious parents to the monastery. He might have showed early that interest in religion and capacity for learning which became so evident later. Or his parents might have died, and his kin might have sent him to the monastery, in its role as an orphanage, for care. Happy or sad, we cannot be sure. But that Bede flourished in the disciplined and cultured life of Benedict Biscop's monastery, and subsequently under the humble, loving and learned care of Abbot Ceolfrid, cannot be doubted.

He was ordained deacon earlier than was usual, at the age of nineteen, and priest at thirty. So far as we know he never travelled further than York or possibly Lindisfarne, but kept the discipline of his monastic vow of stability at Wearmouth-Jarrow. He died in the monastery in 735, in his early sixties, and one of the few records of him is a letter about his death by one of his associates, Cuthbert, who kept vigil with him during his last hours.

Yet Bede was a polymath, who, in what might seem an obscure corner of the north east of England, wrote books that changed his world. These books were in massive demand in the years after his death, they were still being copied in the fifteenth century in places as far afield as Italy, they are still used today, and they still enthrall and entertain. He wrote more biblical commentaries than anything else, collecting the material from the authorities available to him from the early Fathers of the church. He added relatively little to these from his own understanding. Still, these commentaries were the most valuable to him of all his works. In addition, he composed works on Latin grammar and metre for the boys in the monastery, he wrote letters, poetry, biography and hagiography. He wrote at length on the topical controversy in the church, the means of dating Easter, and produced works of geography, history, astronomy and natural science.

## BEDE'S FEET OF CLAY?

Enough has been said of Bede to give a true picture of his genius. He was immensely gifted in the arts and in science. A great story-teller, with a light and imaginative touch. A careful historian, concerned to gather information from as wide a range of sources as possible, and (almost unique for this time in doing so) to acknowledge them. A thoughtful biblical scholar, applying his exposition to his audience with a pastor's sensitivity. Charles Plummer confided to his readers at the end of his Editor's Preface to *Baedae Opera Historica*, his superb edition of Bede's historical works, that he found it 'no light privilege to have been for so long a time in constant communion with one of the saintliest characters ever produced by the church of Christ in this island' during his work on Bede's *Ecclesiastical History*. But, we might think, genius such as Bede's surely cannot have existed without some drawbacks of character or disposition?

There are two aspects of Bede's work that might draw the knowing nod of the cynic. The first and perhaps the least significant is his *Letter to Plegwine* (Text 31). One of the works of Bede's early maturity was a treatise on calculations of time and date, essential for the correct dating of the moveable feasts of the church, especially Easter, but much more than that. But in an episode which Bede characterizes as a disorderly party, in the presence of Bishop Wilfrid, Bede was accused of heresy by a certain monk called David. The name suggests David was a Celt. Bede's reply is the *Letter to Plegwine* of 708, in which the accusation is refuted.

The letter is written in the most acidic irony, and it is absolutely clear that Bede had no regard for the pitiful learning and accomplishments of the monk David. But more seriously, he had even less for the now-aged Bishop himself. Bede is careful in what he says about Wilfrid in his *History*. Sometimes, as for example in his defence of the Roman cause at Whitby, Bede even gives him credit. He talks of him with the conventional reverence for one with a reputation for saintliness. But there is no warmth, and perhaps even an underlying antagonism towards him which colours the way Bede reports events.

There is a great contrast between Wilfrid, whose love of power and wealth reflected the Gaulish and Roman ideal of the prince-bishop, and Cuthbert, whose desire, even as bishop, was to retire to the hardship and remoteness of the hermit life on the Farne Islands. Bede was aware of this contrast. And since Cuthbert was an early enthusiast for the Roman cause and was probably a member of the Roman party before Whitby, Bede found in him a figure combining the best of Celtic discipline with Roman orthodoxy. Wilfrid lacked this discipline, which Bede admired greatly in Cuthbert.

## ATTITUDES TO BRITISH CHRISTIANS

The second aspect of Bede's work that might indicate he had feet of clay, is his attitude to British Christians. Bede's account of the events leading up to and including the Battle of Chester is unquestionably distasteful to anyone influenced by modern ideas of political correctness (Text 25). Bede lived all his life in Bernicia, part of the later and larger kingdom of Northumbria, and he seems to feel closer ties with his heathen compatriots than with his Christian brothers and fellow monks.

But the matter is perhaps more complex than it seems at first sight. Bede was probably using a single main source for his account of the battle and its attendant circumstances, and he may not be entirely to blame for the prejudice expressed. Such attitudes also surface elsewhere in the literature of the period. For example, a writer called Stephen attributes to Bishop Wilfrid far from liberal sentiments. In a passage nothing short of chilling, the biographer records his sermon for the dedication of the church at Ripon in 678:

> Wilfrid stood in front of the altar in the presence of the kings [Ecgfrith and Ælfwine]. Turning to the people, he listed clearly the lands which the kings, for the good of their souls, had previously, and on that very day as well, given to him. [The gifts were made] with the agreement and over the signatures of the bishops and all the chief men. He also listed the holy places in various regions which the British clergy had deserted when fleeing from the hostile sword wielded by the warriors of our own nation. It was indeed a gift pleasing to God that the pious kings had dedicated so many lands to our bishop for the service of God. (*Life of Bishop Wilfrid*, chapter 17)

The 'gift pleasing to God', we may note, included churches wrested from British Christians by bloody force.

Another possibility, and one that seems more consistent with Bede's overriding concerns, is that Bede was attempting to interpret the spiritual implications of a great and bloody battle for the control and overlordship of the whole of Britain. The battle is prefaced in Bede's narrative by the test miracle of the healing of a blind man, in which the British bishops fail where Augustine succeeds (Text 10). The test miracle was a popular motif in medieval saints' lives, but one not much favoured by Bede himself. A given saint proves his or her greater power and sanctity by being able to perform a wonder which another saint, or heathen magician, was unable to. This motif has two broad precedents in scripture. Matthew 17:14f., is where Jesus heals an epileptic boy his disciples could not, and the basic message is that faith is necessary to accomplish miracles. And at 1 Kings 18, where Elijah confronts the prophets of Baal, the message is that faith in the true God is vindicated.

Bede makes it clear that he thinks the British Christians were apostate, having 'despised the offer of everlasting salvation', having twice rejected the truth, preferring their own traditions. And just as four hundred prophets of Baal were taken off and killed after Elijah's God responded to his prayer with a miracle, so in fulfilment of Augustine's prophecy twelve hundred British monks suffered the results of their apostasy by being massacred at the hands of the heathen Northumbrians. It was Bede's conviction that persistence in beliefs and practices not in accordance with catholic doctrine was unjustifiable, and probably meant that anyone guilty of such a thing was less than Christian. The judgement is harsh, no doubt. But Bede believed that history teaches lessons and here he tries to make sense, within the limits imposed by his time and his world view, of historical events.

These two examples of a side of Bede's character that is less than pleasing, reflect his grand obsession with orthodoxy and catholicity. The charge of heresy made by David and not instantly refuted by Bishop Wilfrid was a personal affront to someone of Bede's deep devotion. Bede was strongly partisan on matters like the dating of Easter, what kind of tonsure a monk should have, and issues of ecclesiastical organization. But these were subjects of intense debate in Bede's time. For Bede, and the church of his time, it mattered that the church was united and orthodox in its faith and practice.

## PRAGMATISM

We do not have to agree with Bede. But when we compare his work with that of others, he emerges as more honest than most. He faced up to the most important conflict between Christians in his day, and made his own views clear. But he also faced up to the conflict between his own assumptions and the evidence. Aidan was an admirable and holy person though he would have disagreed with Bede over the critical issue of Easter. Wilfrid, though he publicly argued for everything Bede held dear, was a difficult and contentious person, and Bede acknowledged his own ambivalence towards the man who was his own bishop. Bede was more honest than most of us are about assumptions.

Conflict between Christians is always painful. The Anglo-Saxon church was not the only one to argue over tradition and change. While recognizing the importance of the Celtic influence in their faith, the Anglo-Saxon church nevertheless had the courage to refuse to become a heritage industry. Some beauty was lost, but not truth. Not everything about the way the issue was handled was admirable. But Anglo-Saxon Christianity was spiritually pragmatic in a difficult issue, and chose a way forward that would better equip it to meet the needs of society.

# 6

## CÆDMON AND CÆDMON'S HYMN

## THE STORY OF CÆDMON (TEXT 32)

Bede's *Ecclesiastical History* is divided into five books. The first puts England into a geographical and Christian context, reaching a narrative peak with the first missions to the Anglo-Saxons at the end of the sixth century. These start with the story of Gregory the Great visiting the slave market and seeing the fair-haired English boys, a story mentioned earlier (Text 1). In the second book, the high point is the story of the conversion of Northumbria under King Edwin, with the appearance of Coifi and the retainer who speaks of life as like the flight of a sparrow through the hall (Text 11). In the third book, there is the story of the Council of Whitby in 664 where the two factions, Celtic and Roman, within English Christianity debated what were the correct observances of the orthodox faith (Text 29). In the fourth book, it is the story of Cædmon that sees a further leap forward in the progress of English Christianity, as the faith is preached by means of vernacular poetry. In the last book, the growth and orthodoxy of the English church is confirmed in various miracles, by the increasing numbers of saintly people, in the preaching of the gospel on the continent, and by numerous visions.

We will focus on the story of Cædmon for the rest of this chapter. It is interesting for many reasons. As we have looked at the other narrative peaks of the *History* we have seen Bede's concern to understand the processes that went into Gregory's decision to send a mission to England, Edwin's council's decision to adopt Christianity, and the Whitby decision to back Roman Christianity. Bede tells the stories well, with imagination. He does the same in the story of Cædmon, but here the story is a miracle story. We see Bede interpreting the significance of the story within the development of English Christianity, much as he does in the other stories.

But in the Cædmon story we can see Bede emphasizing the miraculous nature of Cædmon's gift. Not surprisingly, perhaps, the miracle at the centre of the story has been the subject of much dispute, in a way that the other non-miraculous stories have not. Unusually, there is evidence relating to the miracle which does not come either from Bede or directly from his *History*. Most miracle stories consist of healings or visions or unexplainable events, and once the witnesses have gone, there is nothing to encourage belief beyond a personal faith that such things happen. The striking thing about the story of Cædmon is that it is about a divine gift, and there is evidence quite independent of Bede to witness to its reality. Such evidence cannot compel belief, but a miracle remains one of the best explanations.

The story of Cædmon is in the *Ecclesiastical History*, book 4, chapter 24. The events take place during Hild's abbacy at Whitby, before her death in 680. Cædmon, a herdsman, is visited in his sleep by 'someone' and told to sing a song of creation. He has never sung songs before and has avoided the

Anglo-Saxon karaoke parties where songs are sung by people in turn for the entertainment of the company. Cædmon sings a song for his mysterious visitor, and when in due course the abbess and her scholars have heard it, they conclude that Cædmon has been given a divine gift. They take Cædmon into the monastery, and teach him the scriptures. Like a cow making milk out of the grass and cud, Cædmon chews over what he has been taught and turns it into delightful verse, which is instrumental in the conversion of many.

Bede's is the only record of this story. Apart from a couple of references in later literature which borrow from Bede, and an account of the moving of Cædmon's bones, there is no other record of the man. This is not unusual, and shows us again how much we owe to Bede. There are clear signs that Bede saw the story through the standard stereotypes of the time. Cædmon knew he was about to die, for example, and this is a motif from the life of the saint, showing his or her preparedness for the joys of heaven. And the programme of education which Cædmon undergoes in the monastery, and which he uses for his verse, closely matches the educational programme laid out by St Augustine of Hippo in his educational treatise, *De Catechizandis Rudibus*. In other words, Bede is interpreting Cædmon for his audience: Cædmon was close to being a saint, and he followed in the footsteps of those who taught the faith.

We might also note the underlying focus of the story of Cædmon. Cædmon's name is Celtic, and Whitby was known as a monastery favourably disposed towards Celtic ways. Having described in earlier books the missionary success among the English of the great Celtic saints, Aidan in particular, Bede uses this story to show how another saintly man, ethnically Celtic, furthered the gospel by means of his divinely given gift of poetry. At Whitby, the centre of Celtic sentiment, the decision was taken to follow the path of catholicity rather than schism. Similarly at Whitby, a Celt, Cædmon, gave new impetus to the English mission through his use of vernacular English verse.

## CÆDMON AND CONVERSION

In some senses the whole of Bede's *Ecclesiastical History* is about conversion. But this story is particularly so. Bede sees the story as another step in the ongoing process of conversion of the English. There are conversions at the personal level, of Cædmon and others, and there is the conversion of poetry. The first of these conversions is predictable, the second less so.

Cædmon himself is converted progressively. From someone who left parties in case he had to sing, he becomes someone whose verses convert many. He is converted first to be able to sing. Then he is converted to monasticism. And finally he is converted into a saint. We ought to note that Bede quotes Galatians 1:1, in relation to Cædmon's gift. St Paul writes of his apostolic vocation, given to him by God, 'not from man, nor by human means', and Bede makes a similar claim for Cædmon's gift. It means upheaval in his life, just as it did for St Paul, a complete break with what went before. This gift of poetry was a serious gift and vocation that Cædmon received from God. Cædmon did not just retreat into a monastic cell and start writing romantic poems about his feelings. We need to remember that Cædmon was illiterate, and the poet of Anglo-Saxon society exercised a public role. So the gift involved him in public teaching. The Old English translation of Bede's *History* (of which more later) specifically notes that Cædmon's instructors learned from what he spoke and wrote it down. Through Cædmon's gift, he became a kind of apostle to the English.

In the Middle Ages the word *conversion* sometimes referred to the adoption of a monastic vocation, and Cædmon became a monk at Whitby. Once again Bede is at pains to emphasize the reality of this conversion. Cædmon humbly submitted to the regular discipline of the monastery and its Rule, and hotly rebuked those who did otherwise. And at the end, Cædmon's premonition of death is a motif common in the saint's life. Cædmon departed in saintly peace. It was a long journey from herdsman to saint, and few, other than St Patrick before him, made it. But Cædmon managed it.

## THE CONVERSION OF POETRY

Then there is the conversion of poetry. Bede does not actually state that Cædmon's poetry was the first English religious verse, but certainly implies it. 'Others after him tried to compose religious poems in English, but none could compare with him.' And then he gives us the list of Cædmon's compositions, which cover the whole range of biblical and doctrinal topics. Before Cædmon's conversion, Bede implies, there had only been the kind of frivolous and profane songs in the vernacular that Cædmon had refused to sing in the party. After him there was in addition his own poetry and that of his imitators. A whole new tradition sprang up, taking spiritual and moral matters as the proper subject of poetry. Again, Bede is at pains to stress several times over that Cædmon had never learned and did not know any songs before his vision, and that this conversion of poetry was God-given.

Another aspect of the conversion of poetry is the claim that Cædmon's poetry was different in quality, not just in subject-matter, from the kind of songs that were sung at the karaoke party. It is often assumed by scholars that if everybody sang in turn at a party for farm-labourers, the kind of thing they sang would be more like the popular ballad than the heroic tales and praise songs of the king's professional poet. This is a fair assumption. Bede might not be making a great claim for the art of Cædmon's songs if this is what he is comparing it with. But there is a slight difficulty about this, namely that the popular tradition has not been recorded. And indeed, we only have nine lines of poetry that we can with any confidence attribute to Cædmon, his *Hymn*. This makes it rather difficult to verify Bede's claims.

But we can say from the nine lines of Cædmon's *Hymn*, that this is regular, classical poetry of the standard Germanic sort. It uses the alliterative form of all Old English poetry, binding the two halves of the line of verse together by echoing the sounds. The second line of Cædmon's *Hymn* could be fairly literally translated as 'the might of the Measurer, and the thought of his mind', and the m-sounds give the line its structure, rather than rhyme (which was only developed later). And it uses the style of all Old English verse, which echoes concepts in different words to build up a picture. So the last three lines of the *Hymn* can be translated as 'then the Guardian of mankind, the eternal Lord, the Lord almighty, afterwards created the earth, the land for people'. Here we have three different phrases for God, and two for the earth. Given that Old English poetry weaves pictures by this rather indirect process, and that we only have the nine lines of Cædmon's verse to examine, the *Hymn* bears up under examination very well.

Some scholars see the essential miracle of the story of Cædmon as the conversion of the aristocratic poetic tradition to Christian uses. In this view, the original form of verse was the aristocratic praise song, like many poems from Old Norse, and such as is still found in African oral poetry. The theory is that any of the phrases which refer to God could replace secular ones referring to kings or princes. So Cædmon could have replaced a phrase like *eorla dryhten*, 'lord of warriors', with *ece dryhten*, 'eternal Lord'. This theory makes the miraculous element easier to swallow in one way. It suggests that Cædmon's verse had a precedent of sorts and that he could have picked up the formulas from praise songs. Without ever having sung a song, he could still have picked up the formulas, which he later turned to Christian purposes. But in another way it makes nothing easier, because Bede emphasizes that Cædmon was a herdsman. He was therefore unlikely to have been in regular contact with courtly styles of poetry so that he *could* pick up the formulas.

Perhaps a more serious objection to the miraculous origin of Cædmon's verse has come from those who think it is just too ordinary. It follows the norms and conventions of all Old English poetry, and nothing about it is remarkable. Let us look briefly at the illiterate herdsman's verse. These nine lines are all we have, and I have here translated the main West Saxon version:

Now we ought to praise the Guardian of the kingdom of
        heaven,
    the might of the Creator and his understanding,
    the works of the Father of glory, how he, of each wonder,
    the eternal Lord, established a beginning.
He first created for the sons of the earth
heaven as a roof, the holy Creator;
    then the world, the Guardian of humankind,
    the eternal Lord, afterwards created
    the land for the people, the almighty Lord.

At first sight, the repetition and patterning in the phrasing might strike us as crude. But it is quite sophisticated when we look more closely. Take the middle lines for example, 'He first created for the sons of the earth/heaven as a roof, the holy Creator.' Of course a creator creates. But the lines enclose within God's creative nature and activity both earth and heaven, people created from the dust and the roofing vault of the skies. We can see a criss-cross pattern, with the contrast earth-heaven matched and enclosed by the parallel created-Creator. This is a kind of verbal equivalent to the interlace in Anglo-Saxon art, where patterns cross and intertwine.

God is twice referred to as a 'guardian', first of the kingdom of heaven, then of humanity. God is to be praised as the one above all, who in his infinite wisdom was the first cause of every wonder. But that does not make him an impersonal force. His creative activity focused from the first on human-kind, providing first a roof for their heads, then adorning the world for their benefit. He is God not only of the eternal realm, but in time and space he nurtures his creatures. On the other hand, that does not make him subject to time and change: he is 'the eternal Lord', a phrase twice repeated to reinforce this crucial point.

There are echoes of the Bible and liturgy in the poem. The liturgy of the Eucharist reminds us that it is right for human beings to give thanks and praise to God, the almighty and eternal God who created all things from the beginning. The Psalms speak of the heavens declaring the glory of God and the skies proclaiming the work of his hands. The Benedictine Office (service routine) starts several of its daily services with 'We ought to praise God'. Cædmon's *Hymn* seems to reflect and embed these familiar words and ideas within its own development.

When we put all these things together, the *Hymn* ceases to look primitive. It is a poem which teaches subtle theology with simplicity and directness. It uses language that belongs to the Anglo-Saxon poetic tradition, but that also echoes and resonates with the Christian language of the Bible and church services. For the uneducated and unpoetic Cædmon to produce this would indeed be a miracle. Hild's scholars heard a work of unexpected spiritual, theological and artistic depth when they listened to Cædmon's *Hymn*.

## DOUBTS

So, in Bede's story we have a first-rate account of how a single reluctant, obedient, humble and devout man made a difference in the world. But you do not have to be unduly cynical to have the glimmer of a suspicion that the story is almost too good to be true. When Cædmon asks for the Eucharist before he dies, the reply of his companions is just a little bit too much for us to swallow. 'Why do you need the Eucharist? You are not likely to die, since you are talking as cheerfully with us as if you were in perfect health.' Bede is here undoubtedly protesting too much. He might have been trying to cover up the fact that the story was made up. So what evidence is there that the story and its details are true, and is there any good evidence to the contrary?

There are parallels to the story of the conversion of Cædmon almost everywhere, from India to Scandinavia. Bede knew the story of St Jerome, who was accused in a dream of being more Ciceronian than Christian, and who vowed never to touch the frivolous and pagan authors again. There is also a tradition about St Paulinus of Nola, once again known to Bede, in which he was converted from dabbling in profane verse in a dream, and only wrote edifying literature afterwards.

Take away the dream element, and the calling of any of the Old Testament prophets would be some kind of parallel, or the conversion of St Paul likewise. And even the Annunciation, as one scholar has recently suggested, makes a fairly close parallel. The angel appears, tells Mary she is going to have a child, Mary says that it is impossible, the angel insists, and Mary accepts and sings a song. Bede would not have had to look far for a pattern to model the Cædmon story on. But conversion stories, whether religious ones or ones about weight loss or lifestyle changes, always do fit into a pattern, and this can be no reason to disbelieve them in itself.

For the conversion of poetry, recent studies of living oral poets in the Baltics and Africa suggest that competence in oral poetic composition is the result of a long process of learning the traditions and formulas which go into poetic production. Some scholars suggest that Bede's emphasis on the fact that Cædmon knew no songs and was unable to sing is an attempt to disguise the very evidently formulaic nature of his poetry, and thus the long exposure to formulaic verse that must have preceded it. Take the phrase mentioned above, for example. *Ece drihten* occurs eighty-one times in Old English poetry, and twice in the *Hymn*. Few formulas occur more often in Old English poetry. This phrase encapsulated the difference between ordinary lords, who are in the end temporary however great their fame, and the Eternal Lord. Bede would have us believe that this phrase in the *Hymn* is the original which struck other poets as so peculiarly appropriate for God, that they copied it.

We are not really in a position to make a judgement on this matter, but plainly what became a clichéd Christian epithet for God had to come from somewhere. There was a time when *ece drihten* had not been repeated endlessly. Even if it was modelled on a pre-existing phrase (and all language is), Cædmon has as good a claim as anyone to have been the first to use it. The problem with the non-miraculous interpretation of Cædmon's formulaic verse is the one I've mentioned already, that herdsmen do not get invited to many royal banquets and hear the royal praise songs that the *Hymn* is supposed to be based on. And moreover, herdsmen are not often trained in aristocratic versifying. So I'm not personally persuaded to disbelieve Bede's account by the formulaic argument.

## THE PROBLEM OF LANGUAGE

Bede gives us the *Hymn* in Latin. He stresses the English language of Cædmon's poetry and the whole point of the story is that this was a new way of teaching Christian truth. But he does not give the English. If it were not for scribes who knew the *Hymn* from oral tradition writing it into their manuscripts, we would not have an Old English version at all. We can view this in a number of ways. Despite Bede's enthusiasm about the beauty of the work, he might have been embarrassed by the simplicity of it. He might have been simply translating the essentially local and ordinary English into timeless Latin, the language of religion and scholarship. He might not have had access to Cædmon's works, and have felt awkward about giving only a few lines. He might have been thinking about the usefulness of his own work in Europe and elsewhere where Cædmon's dialect of Old English would be meaningless. Whatever we might think, Bede does not give us even a sample of the Old English version.

For many years the suggestion has circulated that Bede does not give us the Old English version because it did not exist. That is, there was no Cædmon, and no *Hymn* before

Bede made them up. Bede strung together a few words which might sound like Old English verse. Then the scribes who copied his work colluded in the deception by glossing or translating the Latin 'back' into Old English. As one scholar has wittily phrased it,

> with all due respect to the memory of Cædmon, it would not have taken a major poet to turn Bede's paraphrase into the *Hymn* that has come down to us ... a glossator with no poetic skills at all would have ended up with about two-thirds of the poem's locutions, all metrically viable ... With Bede's caveat before him about the difficulty of translating poetry word for word, an intelligent glossator familiar with the conventions of Old English poetry could finish the job in *his* sleep.

If Bede's story is true, why did he give only about two-thirds of the poem in Latin and miss out bits here and there? To answer this question, we have to pay attention to what Bede says about the impossibility of transferring the beauties of poetry in one language into another. He invokes very clearly the question of *style*.

## CÆDMON'S HYMN AND STYLE

I have mentioned the two main features of Old English poetic style: echoing sounds to make the link between the two halves of each line (alliteration), and echoing phrases describing different aspects of the same person or thing. This second feature of style is known technically as 'variation'. I have given a fairly literal translation of Cædmon's *Hymn* above. If we then transfer the English translation, now with the variations in square brackets, to Bede's Latin paraphrase, it is immediately apparent what Bede was doing.

Now we ought to praise the Guardian of the kingdom of
    heaven,
    *Nunc laudare debemus auctorem regni caelestis,*
the might of the Creator and his understanding,
    *potentiam creatoris et consilium illius*
the works of the Father of glory, how he, of each wonder
    *facta patris gloriae: quomodo ille miraculorum omnium,*
[the eternal Lord,] established a beginning.
    *cum sit aeternus deus, auctor exstitit,*
He first created for the sons of the earth
    *qui primo hominum filiis*
heaven as a roof, [the holy Creator;]
    *caelum pro culmine tecti* _____
then the world, the Guardian of humankind,
    *dehinc terram humani generis custos*
[the eternal Lord,] afterwards created
    _____ *creauit*
[the land] for the people, [the almighty Lord.]
    _____ *omnipotens.*

Bede was deliberately avoiding the characteristic style of Old English poetry, with its variation and repetition. He omits one variation altogether, he replaces another with a clause (*cum sit...,* 'since he is ...'), and another phrase he changes into an adjective (*omnipotens,* 'the almighty one'). Bede could repeat Latin words with change in meaning (*auctor* is both 'creator' and 'beginning'). But he did not use them in strict repetition as the Old English does (the two examples of 'guardian' are translated *auctor* and *custos*). So Bede has converted the poem into correct Latin prose style. Latin, like modern English, does not readily adapt to the style of Old English verse. But when we put the versions side by side it becomes clear that Bede's concern was to give a correct Latin paraphrase of the verse, not to translate the poem. If he had translated it, it would have been a rather bizarre piece of Latin, and this might well have made Bede's non-English readers doubt Cædmon's ability as a poet.

Bede knew the poem now called Cædmon's *Hymn*, and he simply paraphrased it in his *History* for his Latin readers. We can even see how he did it. When we look at the many manuscripts of Bede's *History*, we cannot see any evidence for the view that scribes 'reconstructed' a *Hymn* from Bede's Latin. There are about 125 complete or partial manuscripts of the work from the medieval period. Only twenty-one of these manuscripts contain an Old English version of the *Hymn*. In every case, the *Hymn* is recognizably the same piece of verse, even when it has changed from the early Northumbrian dialect of Old English of the earliest manuscripts, to late West Saxon, or early Middle English in the latest manuscripts. If scribes had reconstructed the Old English, there would almost certainly be different phrases put into the gaps of Bede's paraphrase. And we would have no reason to suppose that such a made-up poem would get out into the wider world and become a popular piece of verse.

There are two basic groups of manuscripts, those of the *Ecclesiastical History* in Latin and those of the Alfredian translation into Old English. The translation was completed around the end of the tenth century, probably as part of King Alfred's policy of having important educational works translated for those ignorant of Latin. The two groups of manuscripts treat the vernacular *Hymn* differently. In the Latin group the Old

English version of the poem is an addition, a footnote, a marginal annotation. So in the earliest manuscript containing the *Hymn* in Northumbrian Old English, the Moore manuscript of about 737, the poem appears at the end of the book, complete, along with some glosses and other notes. This shows that the Old English Cædmon's *Hymn* always was an addition to Bede's text. In other words, Bede did not compose it.

When the Alfredian translator came to Cædmon's *Hymn* he missed out Bede's passage about the difficulty of rendering poetry in another language, and simply gave the Old English text of the *Hymn* substantially as we find it in the earliest manuscripts. There is one significant difference between the earliest manuscripts and the Alfredian ones. The Alfredian versions have the phrase 'he first created *for the sons of earth* heaven as a roof', and the italicized phrase in Bede and the Northumbrian versions is 'for the sons of men'. In other words, the Alfredian translator knew the *Hymn* in an English form. He was not translating Bede's Latin. All the evidence from the manuscripts confirms the view that Cædmon's *Hymn* was widely known in a strong oral tradition.

## BEDE AND HISTORY

We have trawled deep and wide waters looking at the story of Cædmon. The most important thing here has been to show that a belief in the historical occurrence of miracles is not naïve and mindless credulity. Taking account of all the available evidence, the case against Cædmon's miraculous gift is unproven. The persistence of the arguments seems to be as much a matter of a different *view* of history itself, as of historical evidence. We tend to justify our world view by rewriting history through its assumptions. This raises the question whether there is a

Christian view of history which modern readers might share with Bede and Anglo-Saxon Christians more generally.

Bede was one of the most important medieval English writers. His work was borrowed and added to and plundered by writers in the Middle Ages, and the trend shows no signs of abating even now. Scholars recognize the value of Bede's biblical and exegetical works. They tell us something about the library Bede had at his command, and about the knowledge of Greek in Anglo-Saxon England, for example, apart from giving us an insight into the Anglo-Saxon mind. But the verdict of history has been that Bede's great *Ecclesiastical History* of England, the *Historia Ecclesiastica Gentis Anglorum*, is his outstanding achievement. He finished it in 731, near the end of his life.

Through his work on history and chronology, Bede was instrumental in popularizing the Dionysian system of dating. This is the dating system that is used in the west now, the BC/AD system which sees the turning point of universal history as the birth of Christ, and calculates years before and after his birth. Earlier calculations were based on years of kings, or popes, complex and confusing methods that could only be useful locally or to the learned. Bede's gift for clarity is nowhere better seen than in the adoption of this simple device, and it argues a serious attitude to the subject of history and the science of historiography. This dating system provides an adequate framework for the consideration of the history of England as part of a much greater whole. Not many people thank Bede for his work on the dating of Easter mentioned in the previous chapter, but we would be in desperate trouble without some such system as the BC/AD one.

The modern reader of Bede's *History* will, however, immediately be struck by the fact that it is peppered with miracle stories, like the one related of Cædmon. Moreover, like his predecessors who wrote the great church histories, Eusebius and before him St Luke, Bede had a religious and moral purpose to writing. He writes in his preface to the *History*,

> If history records good things of good men, the thoughtful hearer is encouraged to imitate what is good: or if it mentions evil of wicked men, the pious, religious listener or reader is encouraged to avoid all that is sinful or perverse, and to follow what he knows to be good and worthy of God.

At the same time, Bede made greater efforts than most to verify his information, to use reliable informants, to quote authorities with discrimination and to name his sources.

Bede tried first of all to find out the details, and then to interpret the significance of his material for his readers. His purpose was never to distort the evidence, but to use it selectively. Indeed, I think it is clear that he *understood* the evidence selectively. What results is as far from dreary moralizing as can be imagined: lively narrative, colourful characters, fast-paced action, believable dialogue anchored by verifiable historical fact and plausible explanation. Though he records many wonder stories, his first reaction to such tales is not 'wow!' but 'why?' God is a God of order, and though he may not always disclose his purposes, there is a pattern to his working. The idea that God works in mysterious ways did not deter Bede from trying to understand the why and the how.

Bede was a fine historian, remarkable by modern standards let alone those of his time. His methods were rigorous. Christian history was not gullibility, but a researched discipline. It is only in recent years that the dominant view of history as an unbiased record of absolute fact has lost ground to the view that history involves selection and interpretation of evidence. Bede knew and practised this in the eighth century. There are miracles in Bede, but they are there because he understood them as part of God's work in the world. Bede set them within the pattern of a steady advance in Christianity. There are points at which we will inevitably disagree with Bede. But in most ways he models a careful, scholarly, Christian approach to history.

## TAKING A BROAD VIEW ...

There are all kinds of issues raised by the story of Cædmon. We have looked at a wide range of evidence relating to the story and the preservation of the *Hymn*. Taking a broad view, none of the objections raised by recent studies to the miraculous nature of Cædmon's gift are conclusive. A reasonable investigation of the evidence, indeed, supports the view that Bede's account is substantially true. Doubtless the story has been 'improved' in the course of its journey from the community at Whitby to Bede. Doubtless, too, Bede used his unique story-telling gifts to the full in the narrative. But without something remarkable happening, Cædmon would not have been remembered at all, let alone as the faithful, humble herdsman who taught the faith in delightful verse. The great pity is we have no more of his verse than the *Hymn*.

I have taken Bede's cue in investigating the story of Cædmon. It is important to enjoy the story and learn its lesson that God's gifts can utterly transform a person's life. But it is equally important not to be credulous and impressed only with the marvellous. The miracle story appeals as much to reason and a sense of pattern and purpose in God's works as it does to wonder and a sense of the supernatural. The truly fascinating thing is that Cædmon's Hymn is all about discerning purpose in miracle. In the Hymn, Cædmon's patterned language reflects patterns in the creative work of God. The miracle of creation in Cædmon's life enables him to respond to the miracle of creation.

But a further purpose to the miracle is evident in the story of Cædmon. His personal experience enabled him to communicate better with others. His skill in poetry was a spiritual gift, but Cædmon had to practise it. His conversion involved rejection of some things, certainly, but growing excellence in others. The miracle of his conversion was worked out in everyday life. Once again, Anglo-Saxon Christianity recognized the value of pragmatic, grounded, worked out, thoughtful spirituality.

# 7

# BEOWULF

## ORTHODOX VIEWS OF THE
## UNCONVERTED HEATHEN

In an earlier chapter we looked at Alcuin's letter to Higbald of Lindisfarne, berating the brethren for listening to heroic tales (Text 20). Heathen kings are in hell, Alcuin says, and it is therefore wholly improper for monks to listen to stories about them. Bede's view that before Cædmon, *all* vernacular verse was profane and unprofitable might also be mentioned (Text 32). This view is not so extreme, but tends the same way. Alcuin makes it quite clear that he is orthodox and August-inian in his doctrine on the salvation of the heathen. Early in the fifth century, St Augustine of Hippo effectively made baptism the sign and seal of salvation and entry into the Church. He coined the neat phrase, *extra ecclesiam nulla salus*, 'outside the church there is no salvation'. Whatever you or I may think of such a maxim, it was the classic rule of thumb for the medieval church.

In Anglo-Saxon society your genealogy was like a personal identity card, the extended clan group was the basis of social security and stability, and your own name, the name of your settlement and your tribal name, every time you used them, would very probably remind you of your past and your links with, and your indebtedness to, those who had gone before. In such a society, it was inevitable that there would be those who felt and thought differently from the great authoritative Father of the Church – even when society was Christian by conviction and orthodox by habit. But orthodoxy is nearly always by definition the view of the powerful. So how should doubt about it be expressed? How could a distinctly Germanic and distinctly Christian reservation about the accepted doctrine of the Church be framed? And what hope could be given to people who felt it to be a duty to keep the memory of their ancestors alive?

Alcuin's letter puts the orthodox view clearly and powerfully, and similarly orthodox views could be illustrated a hundred times over. Alcuin wrote his letter at the end of the eighth century. The time was one of huge evangelistic effort in northern and central Europe. Sometimes it is difficult to disentangle religious imperialism from dynastic imperialism, particularly among the predecessors of Charles the Great (Charlemagne), for whom Alcuin was working. But in the circumstances the orthodox view of salvation was a very strong incentive to missionary endeavour. Alcuin was personally in a situation where heathen nonsense was getting in the way of evangelization and the educational work he had been appointed to do.

But it has not often been noticed that one of the main reasons Alcuin expressed the view so forcefully, with all the rhetorical echoes and flourishes that we observed, was because he believed that the Lindisfarne brethren might disagree. There were Celtic theologians who outlined a more liberal notion of the fate of the unconverted heathen, in relation to a theory of natural revelation and innate goodness. These writers would probably be known at Lindisfarne, itself an Irish foundation. I am not referring here in particular to Pelagius, the great teacher of the heretical doctrine that people could be saved by their own efforts. But the fact is that Pelagius was one of a company of thinkers of Celtic origins who begged to differ from the apparently harsh orthodoxy.

## A GOOD HEATHEN

Apart from some rather obscure Celtic theological texts, one of the most telling instances of the difficulty ordinary people experienced with this doctrine comes from the late fourteenth-century poem, *St Erkenwald*. Eorcenwald, to whom the poem refers, was the fourth bishop of London; he was born about 630 and died in 693. The story is told that in the building of the church of St Paul's in London, the masons uncovered a sarcophagus. When it was opened, there was revealed an uncorrupted corpse in splendid clothes. Erkenwald commanded it to speak and explain itself, and the corpse related how, when it was alive, it was a heathen judge, righteous and just in every way. Because this judge was just and incorruptible according to his lights when alive, his body had remained incorrupt. His soul, however, was in limbo awaiting judgement at the Last Day, because he was ignorant of Christ and was never baptized. The corpse laments the darkness in which it lies, when it now knows the truth of Christ's sacrifice and grace.

All the masons and people around feel desperately sad for the fate of the just man. Erkenwald is moved to tears, and thinks of the desperate expedient of fetching holy water and baptizing the corpse to release it from its misery. Just then, a tear falls from his face on to the body, and with a song of praise to God and thanks to the saint, the body dissolves as the soul departs to bliss:

> Now may you, the high God, and your gracious mother, be
> given praise,
> And blessed be the blissful hour she bore you.
> And may you be blessed, Bishop, who banished my grief,
> And relieved my soul from the loathsome gloom of her
> life!
>
> For the sentence you spoke, and the sprinkling of water,
> The bright brook of your tears, brought about my baptism:
> The first drop that fell finished all my woe.
> Now my soul may be seated at the supper table.
>
> For with the words and the water that wash away pain,
> A gleaming light flashed low in the abyss,
> So that my spirit sprang swiftly to unstinted joy
> To the feast where all the faithful feed in fine solemnity.

Bede mentions several miracles of Eorcenwald's, including one where a wheel falls off his carriage, but the carriage still rolls on and gets him to his destination. But Bede does not mention this one, which might suggest it is a late tradition. The striking thing about it, however, is that it deals with just the sort of questions newly Christianized people might ask. What about the fate of the good heathen? Can only Christians be saved? And the answers it gives are just the kind of ambiguous 'justice tempered by mercy' reply that at one and the same time emphasize the justice of God, the rightness of church doctrine, but the possibility of exceptions to the rule. The people of London at the time of the historical Eorcenwald were just being converted. These would be the sort of questions they were asking. So either the poet imaginatively entered into the historical situation, or was dealing with a tradition that we only know from this poem.

## BEOWULF (TEXT 33)

I want to propose that the poem *Beowulf* is an attempt to answer the same kind of questions: 'what about the good heathen?', and, 'can only Christians be saved?' And more than that, it is an exploration of how the audience of the poem, as Germanic warriors and Christians, could reconcile their status and faith; how they could both honour their past and learn something for their present. With these questions and ideas in mind, I think we can make sense of the poem, both in what it says and in what it does not say.

The story is simple enough. The successful Danish king, Hrothgar, builds a hall called Heorot, and entertains his warriors with singing and feasting. A man-like monster from the fens, Grendel, is disturbed by the feasting and starts to ravage the hall, devouring and carrying off Hrothgar's men. This goes on for twelve years, to the misery and horror of the Danes, who try all kinds of expedients against Grendel. In their desperation, they turn to idols and sacrifices, the hope of the heathen. In due course, Beowulf hears of the problem in the hall of King Hygelac of the Geats in the south of Sweden. Hrothgar had helped Beowulf's father in a blood-feud in years past, so Beowulf sees these incursions of Grendel as an opportunity to repay Hrothgar for his kindness. With a select group of men, Beowulf sails to Denmark, and is welcomed by Hrothgar. After suitable entertainment, and some quite serious argument instigated by a character called Unferth, about whether Beowulf is quite as wonderful as he claims, everybody goes to bed.

Grendel comes creeping from the dark wastelands to the hall where the warriors are sleeping, an eerie light in his eyes. The doors of the hall are like paper at the touch of his hands, and he hungrily reaches for one man and gobbles him down, then reaches for another. This one grabs back at him though, and a great wrestling match ensues, in which Beowulf wrenches Grendel's arm off his body. And Grendel retreats, howling, to the wilderness to die. Sadness and triumph are mixed in the celebration that follows, and heroic tales are told at the banquet. Grendel's arm is nailed up on the wall as a trophy, gifts are given to Beowulf, and in due course everyone goes to bed. In the night, enraged and intending vengeance for her son's death, comes Grendel's mother, more savage even than her son. She snatches one of Hrothgar's closest confidants, and runs off. When morning comes, all Hrothgar's misery returns, because he knows that there is more than one man-eating monster abroad. And now that the idea is forced upon them, men recall that there was talk of two horrid shapes wandering the marshes. And there is a foul pool which always has the dank and hideous dead feel of winter about it, avoided by all animals.

Following the trail of blood, Beowulf and his men get to the pool, and Beowulf decides to dive in to get at the monster. Swimming down, he finds a chamber and wrestles with Grendel's mother. Stronger than her son, she is getting the better of him and is about to stab him, when he sees a huge sword on the wall. He grabs this and hacks at her neck with it. She is now dealt with, with God's help, and Beowulf then finds the body of Grendel, and uses the sword to decapitate him. The sword dissolves in the caustic blood. All the blood that has been spread about has by this time got into the water. And since no Beowulf appears, the men up at the surface think he must be dead. Leaving Beowulf's men to watch, the Danes go off. After a while up pops Grendel's head out of the water, with Beowulf holding it. It takes four of them to carry it back to the hall, where once again, there is much rejoicing. Beowulf is given lots more presents. But since he has been so successful, Hrothgar also gives him some friendly advice about avoiding the pitfalls of pride. With final courtly exchanges, Beowulf returns home, laden with gifts and honours.

In a famous and unsuccessful raid on Frisia, Beowulf's uncle and lord Hygelac is killed. In due course, Beowulf is made king and rules for fifty years, in which he establishes peace and secures the land against all attackers. But a runaway slave breaks into the barrow of a dragon and steals a cup from the treasures, disturbing the dragon. It starts to go on raids, burning and destroying the land. The ageing Beowulf decides he has to do something about this, so he has an iron shield made, chooses eleven men to go with him, and attacks the dragon at its barrow. The dragon's venom and fire are nearly overpowering him. And seeing the danger the chosen men, all but Wiglaf, run off. Wiglaf stabs the dragon in its belly and between them, he and Beowulf kill it. Beowulf is now dying and asks to be given sight of the dragon's treasure, which he has won for his people. He seems to think it is quite a bargain that he has got for them, swapping an old king for lots of gold. A messenger goes off to tell the news that the king is dying, and there are all kinds of gloomy predictions about what all the surrounding enemies will do now. Beowulf's people kick the dragon over the edge of the cliff, and give Beowulf a splendid funeral pyre, burying with him in a huge mound all the gold from the dragon's hoard.

# A STORY FROM HEATHEN TIMES

It is a great story, skilfully told. The setting throughout is heathen, with a ship-cremation at the beginning, heathen sacrifice, and subsequent funeral pyres. We cannot be sure that in
every detail the poet has recorded what heathens did or would
have done. But for much of his information, he probably drew
on pre-existing tradition, and for the rest, he plausibly reconstructed details from what he had seen and heard. Several
episodes in the poem can be dated with some reliability from
the evidence of other sources. Hygelac's raid on Frisia is mentioned by Gregory of Tours in his *History of the Franks*, where
his name is recorded as Chlochilaicus. The raid took place in
the 520s, and at this time the Danes and the Geats (Beowulf's
tribe) were heathen. The wars of the Geats with the Swedes
mentioned in the poem can also be dated to the early years of
the sixth century.

The pre-Christian heroic code of the Germanic peoples
which survived into Christian Anglo-Saxon England is found
at every turn and is heard in the proverbial maxims. Beowulf
tells Hrothgar after Grendel's mother has carried off one of his
warriors, 'It is better for every man that he avenge his friend
than mourn too much.' And towards the end of the poem,
Wiglaf says, before risking his life to help Beowulf, 'Death is
better for every warrior than a life of shame.' These two maxims more or less summarize the heroic code. Loyalty is based
on the obligations of the warband, concern for personal honour and reputation, and personal commitment to vengeance. It
is a law of action, of force, of blood and guts.

# BENEATH THE SURFACE

So at the surface, there is a great deal of historical verisimilitude. The poet seems to be a sensitive antiquarian, accurately recreating the inherited traditions with both sympathy and imagination. But there are all kinds of things about the poem that force us to think more deeply about what the poet is saying. When we dive into the pool, we find a different world. Take the two maxims just mentioned. Beowulf says the one about vengeance directly to Hrothgar: 'Don't mourn, wise warrior: it's better for every man that he avenge his friend than mourn too much.' But the whole purpose for Beowulf being there in Heorot is that Hrothgar and all his men have proved totally powerless to avenge themselves. That better alternative is not possible for them. What use are heroic maxims to a broken and helpless old man? And Wiglaf spurs himself on at the dragon-fight with a maxim that reminds him not to care about his life, that death is better than shame. The fact that ten picked men have just run away, preferring shame to possible horrible death, may not impinge on Wiglaf's heroic consciousness, but we cannot help noticing it.

Other things similarly force us to think about what the poet is saying. We noted from Tacitus and the Anglo-Saxon settlement of Britain, that the way of life of the Germanic tribes and their warbands was predominantly predatory warfare, attacking other tribes and robbing their goods and cattle rather than making and farming one's own (Text 12). When we come to *Beowulf*, we notice that the hero, as king, establishes peace and prosperity. And along with the very heroic virtues that his retainers wish to praise him for, his nobility, his great deeds of valour and his desire for glory, they also praise his kindness and gentleness. These are not the traits of a typical Germanic hero. We also notice that the exploration of the tension between conflicting duties and loyalties, such as the heroic poets enjoyed, is all pushed to one side. It is there in the so-called digressions, especially in the story of Finn and Hengest, but the main action of the poem is very simple and heroic in a relatively monochrome way. Beowulf does not fight against human beings for the most part, but against monsters: the fen monsters Grendel and his ghoulish mother in the first part, and later in the poem against the dragon. It is a simple opposition of good against evil.

Then we might notice that the heathen characters use the common vocabulary of religion. When Hrothgar has built his hall, his poet sings of the creation, a song with some parallels in Cædmon's *Hymn*. The characters regularly, indeed religiously, give thanks to God for protection and deliverance. When Hrothgar gives his exhortation to Beowulf about the danger of pride, he uses the image of an enemy shooting arrows that harm the soul, clearly borrowed from St Paul's Epistle to the Galatians, chapter 6. When the poet explains the origin of the fen monsters, he invokes the giants and the Flood of Genesis, claiming that the Grendel family derive from the kin of Cain, the first fratricide. Grendel himself is described as 'enemy of God', 'enemy of humanity', 'bearer of God's wrath', 'enemy or fiend from hell', 'captive of hell', and so on, all biblical and Christian designations of the devil or the damned. Some have argued that the dragon is 'that ancient serpent, who is the devil and Satan' mentioned in the book of Revelation, but this is nowhere made explicit, and personally I find it unconvincing: the dragon carries no great theological overtones, but is a figure of irrational aggression. When Grendel heads off, howling, to die, we are told he goes off to await the great Judgement, and the details imply that where he goes is the place of 'darkness, weeping and gnashing of teeth'. We might also notice, however, that despite all this religious language, there is no mention whatever of Christ or the Holy Spirit, the saints or the Church, or any of the essential doctrines of salvation, such as slip easily into other poems.

So on the one hand we have datable and verifiable historical fact, and plausible reconstruction of a bygone era and its rituals. On the other hand there is somewhat anachronistic religiosity, and a storyline anchored in an essentially biblical, Christian world view. This has puzzled scholars over the years, and they have come up with various theories to explain it. Popular at one time was the notion that the poem had been edited from a heathen epic, and a 'monkish redactor' exercised his skills on it. He just added a few bits and took out a few bits and substituted others. Another theory was that the poet was an ignorant, or half-educated Christian who did not know enough of the Bible to get in the most important bits. Or that the religious phrases were culled from commonplaces in sermons or the liturgy. Or that his religious curriculum had only got as far as Genesis, or at best the Old Testament, when the poet was composing the poem. Finally, if the poet was not heathen or half-Christian, the other alternative had to be that he was fully Christian, and that the poem was *really* an allegory of salvation. I cannot do justice to the subtlety of the arguments advanced in support of these theories in the space available. There are anthologies of *Beowulf* criticism in which these views are represented. But for all their subtlety, it seems to me that they are quite mistaken.

## HISTORICAL FANTASY

The poet is consciously using historical fiction to explore the implications of Christian doctrine. To do that, he posits the existence of good and honourable people, with the same religious instincts as his own, but without the knowledge of the gospel of Christ. Such people honour God as Creator and Sustainer of the world, as powerful and active in the world, and as Judge of deeds. They see God as over against the forces of chaos and darkness abroad in the world, and opposed to the workers of evil, the kin-slayers and the monsters. Now in order to pose the question, 'what about such good and honourable people, whose only real fault is that they have not heard the gospel of Christ?', the poet has to sidestep ethical difficulties surrounding war and feud in Anglo-Saxon England. There would be some who would not see the essential righteousness of people who killed a lot. King David was not allowed by God to build a temple for worship because of this very problem. So although the poet knew the quintessentially heroic stories of the North, the stories of Ingeld, and Finn and Hengest, of Weland, of Sigemund the dragon-slayer and the others, and he knew also of the wars and raids and reprisals that went on between Geats and Swedes and Danes and Heathobards, he chose to concentrate on monster stories. Monsters allow a clear-cut distinction between good and evil, and Beowulf can represent unambiguous good in his fight with the Grendels.

It is worth observing at this point that the poet did not invent the stories he used. To the indignation of some early scholars he used folk-tale monster stories. There is a tale-type known as 'the bear's son tale', which is known from over two hundred variants, assembled and discussed by a German scholar called Panzer. The story is very substantially that related in the first part of *Beowulf*:

A demon appears at night in a house which has been built by an aged king. The elder sons of the king are

unable to cope with the intruder, but the youngest one
successfully gets hold of him. The demon is wounded
but manages to get away. A bloody trail shows the way
to his abode ... The hero fights in a strange place,
which in a great many instances is under the earth,
against one or two demons (often a male and a female
one). By this successful exploit he frees several maidens, who are then safely restored to the upper world.
But he himself is betrayed by his faithless companions
and must remain in the realm of the monsters, until he
finds a means of escape ...

Beowulf does not get the maidens. Treasure has to be enough
for him. But for the rest, the pattern is close in every way to the
first part of *Beowulf*. There are parallels to the tale in the Old
Norse saga of Grettir, for example. Beowulf also shows bear-like
characteristics, not only his name 'bee-wolf', which might
mean 'bear', but also his great strength, by which he hugs a warrior to death at one point. Again there is a parallel to this in the
Old Norse saga of Hrolfr Kraki, where there is a character
called Bothvarr Bjarki ('little bear') whose parents are called
Bjorn ('bear') and Bera ('she-bear'), and who takes the form of
a bear in battle. The link with the story of Beowulf is made the
stronger by the fact that Hrolfr, the king's name, is the Norse
form of Old English Hrothulf, who is named in the poem as
nephew of Hrothgar. It is probable then, that the poet was
exploiting the stock characters and situations of popular tales.

# THEOLOGY

The poet has made a dignified, heroic and elegiac poem from
some elements that are less than noble in their origins. But for

his theological purpose, he could not just pose the question, 'What about the righteous heathen?', obvious though it might seem. He needed some biblical basis for questioning the Augustinian consensus. And he found it in St Paul's Epistle to the Romans, chapters 1 and 2. Here Paul writes of natural revelation, that God's nature is revealed through what he has made. But Paul argues that people lost the knowledge of God and worshipped idols. But those who consistently do good will be granted eternal life in the judgement, because in the absence of knowledge of the law of God, they nevertheless do what God requires, and so become 'a law unto themselves'. The poet echoes this passage closely and frequently in the early stages of the poem, so as to establish it as the context in which the action takes place. When Grendel starts his mischief, for example, the Danes turn to idolatry, which is roundly condemned. But the Danes are also pitied:

> Such was their habit,
> the hope of the heathen. They thought of hell
> in their hearts. They did not know the Lord,
> the Judge of deeds, they were not acquainted with the Lord
>     God,
> and did not know how to worship him, the Guardian of
>     the heavens
> and Lord of glory.

Here idolatry and ignorance of the true God are closely related, very much as in the Romans passage.

Having posed the question and raised the issue, the poet gets on with his tale. There are only a few rather ambiguous indicators of what his own views were on the topic. Unferth, the devil's advocate who tests Beowulf on his arrival at Heorot, has a stinging retort from the hero, who corrects his mistaken account of one of his exploits. Beowulf adds,

> You killed your own brothers,
> near relatives – for that you will endure
> damnation in hell, even though you are witty enough.

We are told that those who persist in evil will thrust their souls into hell, that Grendel was always a denizen of hell, and that hell received him when he died. From this, it is clear that hell is the ultimate sanction for those who murder and destroy and persist in wickedness.

For those who are good, there is ambiguous hope. One of the most tender and elegiac passages in the poem is about King Hrethel. Hrethel was Hygelac's father, and his eldest son Herebeald was killed by his younger son, Hæthcyn, in a hunting accident. This raises again the question of what an old man is to do when for reasons beyond his control he cannot carry out vengeance. Hrethel dies of grief, rather than punish his son, and the poet says of him,

> he gave up the joys of men and chose God's light;
> he left his sons, as does a wealthy man,
> his land and his people's stronghold, when he departed this
> life.

Light has always been an image of heaven and glory, and though the verb 'choose' is one that is often used in a rather vague way when there is little or no choice involved, nevertheless Hrethel's decision is undoubtedly seen as a positive one. The word for 'wealthy' is also ambiguous, meaning 'blessed' in the sense of Latin *beatus*. Throughout the Old

English Psalms, the frequently occurring 'blessed' as in 'blessed is the man ...' is invariably translated *beatus* in Latin and *eadig* in Old English.

Beowulf's end is ambiguous in many ways. There are dark murmurings about the mess he has landed his people in, and the uselessness of the treasure he has gained. But just as in the saint's life, his last minutes and words are recorded. He says to Wiglaf, after giving him his arms and armour as a parting gift,

> 'You are the last survivor of our family line,
>   of the Wægmundings. All my kinsmen
>   have been swept away to their destiny by events,
>   brave and noble men. I must follow them.'
> That was the old man's final word,
>   the thoughts of his heart, before he chose the death-pyre,
>   the hot murderous flame. From his breast
>   the soul departed to seek the judgement of the righteous.

There has been much discussion of the phrase *secean sothfæstra dom*, 'to seek the judgement of the righteous', as to precisely what it means. *Dom*, for example, can mean 'praise' as well as 'judgement', 'glory' as well as 'decree'. What does not seem to me to be ambiguous is the contrast between the flames Beowulf's body is to be consigned to, and the much more benign destination of his soul. The poet is far from explicit, but he uses the predominant image of hell, the flames, as the fate of the body, and an image of heaven, the place of the just and righteous, for the destination of the soul. In other contexts, *sothfæst* is a word used of God himself and the saints. God is the righteous one, and the saints are the righteous ones. The poet does not commit himself to the notion that Beowulf gets to heaven, but again, *secean* usually implies not only seeking but finding. If the Christian audience were so disposed, they could hear the poet saying that Beowulf's soul was going to the glory of the saints.

# THEORY AND REALITY

This strikes me as finely contrived ambiguity. Philosophical theory and dogma are both tested by the ambiguity of extreme examples and experience. The poet leaves us and his audience to conclude what we want to conclude from the Germanic experience he has laid before us. He has distanced the action from his immediate audience by using characters and situations from the past, from distant lands, and from folk-tale. He has used fantasy fiction, in fact, to explore this pressing theological question of the salvation of the righteous heathen. He has come to no bland, all-inclusive conclusions, but has given hints that he thinks there is space in heaven for good heathens. And as in the best fantasy, the story is as important as the question from which it starts, and is told with skill and imaginative power. It is this kind of story and this kind of complex theological issue that informs the fantasy of J. R. R. Tolkien and C. S. Lewis. In order to explore the theological and Christian issues I have hardly done justice to the story. You will just have to read it for yourself.

# 8

# THE WAY OF THE CROSS:
# OLD ENGLISH RELIGIOUS POETRY
# AND THE DREAM OF THE ROOD

## CHRISTIAN POETRY

*The Dream of the Rood* is by common consent one of the most moving and powerful poems in Old English. It is a dream vision, in which the cross of Jesus tells its own story to a dreaming man. The cross depicts itself as a loyal retainer of its lord, who nevertheless becomes implicated in its lord's death. The poem explores the tensions of obedience and loyalty, the paradox of victory through apparent defeat. More than that, it makes a contribution to the theological understanding of the incarnation and crucifixion for the Anglo-Saxons. We will explore the poem in more detail later. To put the poem in a wider context, however, and to understand it more fully, we need to take a panoramic view of Old English religious poetry.

The point is worth making at the beginning of this chapter, that *all* Old English poetry is in some sense Christian poetry, but not all of it is religious poetry. There is no truly heathen Old English verse. From the time of the conversion onwards, writing was the province of the educated upper classes, and education and literacy were entirely in the hands of the Church. Thus, although the Church did not immediately and utterly revolutionize the oral traditions of the Anglo-Saxons, it did determine very effectively what was preserved for posterity. So, not surprisingly, the Anglo-Saxon poetry that we have is predominantly religious and aristocratic. Or, to put it another way, it is most frequently Christian *and* heroic. In this matter it represents the coming together of Anglo-Saxon culture and Christian faith, the dressing of the Christian body in Germanic clothes.

Looking at Old English poetry in general, it is evident that by far the greatest quantity of verse in terms of numbers of lines, is religious. For simplicity we can divide poems up into groups, namely biblical poems, saints' lives, liturgical poems and miscellaneous shorter homiletic or didactic verse. Perhaps I should make the point here that by 'homiletic and didactic' I do not mean what most critics currently seem to mean, that these poems are dull and tedious. Some of them undoubtedly lack sparkle, but some on the other hand are among the best and most studied from the Old English period. As we glance through the religious verse of Anglo-Saxon England, we see the consistent assimilation of the heroic and Christian, that process of assimilation which enabled the poet of *The Dream of the Rood* to recreate the crucifixion in theological and heroic terms.

## BIBLICAL POEMS

Among the biblical poems, there are Old English versions of Genesis, Exodus, Daniel (and the related poem called *Azarias*) and the inter-testamental book of Judith. In the *Genesis*, Satan is portrayed as a Germanic warrior chief, who because of his rebellion against his lord, God, is condemned to exile in hell.

Interestingly, this poem incorporates within it a poem from the newly converted Germanic people of the Old Saxons, who lived in an area of what is now Germany. It departs considerably from the biblical text. At the time when this poem was composed, the Old Saxons were in political turmoil, and Satan is depicted as an upstart and traitor. Presumably the poet intended the audience to learn not to switch allegiances wantonly. Here is Satan's speech, as he ponders his great rebellion:

> 'Why should I struggle?', he said. 'I do not need
> one bit to have a lord. I can do just as many miracles
> with my hands. I have great power,
> and can prepare a better throne,
> higher in heaven. Why must I serve to gain his favour,
> grovel to him with allegiance like that? I can be God just
>      as well as he.
> Strong retainers will stand by me, who will not fail me in
>      the battle,
> brave-hearted heroes. They, brave warriors, have chosen
>      me
> as their lord ...'

For the modern reader the difficulty here may be to feel the horror of this as the original audience must have felt it. This kind of rebellion against a gracious lord was utterly at odds with all the culture stood for. Truly devilish.

## SAINTS' LIVES

Saints' lives such as *Andreas*, *Elene*, *Juliana* and *Guthlac*, tend to be translations of Latin sources. Juliana, the heroine of the poem of the same name, undergoes all kinds of tortures for her faith but remains steadfast. She is whipped and ordered to be put in a cauldron of boiling lead, amongst other things. She has a long argument with a demon, but she finally gains the crown of martyrdom when she is beheaded. The demon gloats over what he does to those susceptible to his deceits. But he is forced to tell what happens when he is resisted:

> If I should encounter with a storm of arrows
> any courageous champion of God renowned for bravery,
> a champion who has no wish to flee
> far away from the battle, but wise of heart,
> raises in response a shield, the holy shield
> and spiritual armour, a champion who has no desire to
>      abandon God,
> but rather, bold in prayer, takes his stand
> firmly in the army – I have to make an ignominious retreat
> from there, deprived of pleasures,
> into the grasp of the fiery coals to mourn my misery,
> in that I could not, through my own strength
> prevail in the battle.

The passage is a tissue of biblical references, echoing most of all James 4:7, 'Resist the devil and he will flee from you', but there is also reference to the 'armour of God' passage in Ephesians 6. The boundaries between physical and spiritual warfare are not at all clearly defined here. The fiery arrows of the evil one and the shield of faith merge with the arrows and shields that were the everyday necessities of life in Anglo-Saxon England. In many ways, St Paul's words had more immediacy for the Anglo-Saxons than they do for us.

# LITURGICAL POETRY

Liturgical poetry includes versions of the Lord's Prayer, the Gloria, the Advent antiphons, and the Psalms. *The Lord's Prayer* begins,

> *Pater noster*
> You are our Father, ruler of all,
> the king in glory.

The original idea, that God is a Father, and not only that, but *our* Father, stressing the intimacy of that relationship, has been added to. God is also our powerful ruler, the King to whom we owe allegiance. For the Anglo-Saxons, this would not diminish the intimacy between the Christian and God. They did not have the awe for distant and powerful royalty that the passage might suggest to us. Rather, it images the relationship between the Christian and God as one of the most fundamental and intimate that the Germanic world knew: that between a retainer and his lord.

A poetic version of the Creed has this passage:

> *Tertia die resurrexit a mortuis*
> After the third day the lord of the nations,
> the kingdom's master, rose swiftly from the earth,
> and for forty days with close counsels
> cheered his followers, and then he went
> to seek his kingdom, his heavenly home,
> saying that he would not ever abandon
> anyone who desired to follow him thenceforth,
> who with a devoted heart wished to do his will.

The resurrection and Jesus' ascension discourse at the end of Matthew's gospel, echoed here, is adapted to the pattern of the lord claiming his kingdom and taking allegiance from his men. Once again the intimacy of the relationship is set forth in the image of a lord and his retainers, though perhaps there is more here of the lord's care for his followers than is usual in heroic texts.

## MISCELLANEOUS POEMS

'Miscellaneous' has to be the word. There are several lyrics with Christian teaching, such as *The Wanderer* and *The Seafarer*. There are riddles; charms – both medical and other (e.g. for unproductive land); allegories such as *The Phoenix* and *The Whale*, the former translated and adapted from a Latin poem by Lactantius; poems called *Judgement Day* or *Soul and Body*; didactic works with titles like *The Order of the World*; and more translations, for example, of poems from Boethius' *Consolation of Philosophy*. The vast majority of these are overtly Christian. Only the charms, which are largely heroic in style (stitch is a little spear, bees are victory-women, *sigewif*) show any serious signs of knowledge of a heathen world view. Even then, most of them introduce Christ, or Christian names, or prayers as part of the charm's incantation and ritual.

The *Seafarer* most famously, and most delicately, transforms the heroic concept of immortal fame into a Christian concept of life after death:

> For every warrior, therefore, the praise of the living,
> those who speak of him afterwards, is best.
> [This praise] he can bring about before he must depart on
>     his way

by noble deeds against the malice of enemies
by brave actions against the devil,
so that the sons of men praise him thereafter,
and his praise endures among the angels
for ever and ever, in the glory of eternal life,
bliss among the heavenly company.

All kinds of wordplay can be seen here. For example, the word translated 'enemies' is *feond* and it can also mean 'fiends, demons'. This makes for an ambiguity where the poem could be understood to be saying that physical fighting against enemies can earn heavenly reward, just as much as spiritual 'brave actions against the devil'. Similarly, 'the heavenly company' is a translation of *duguth* which in heroic poetry means the tried and tested older warriors in the warband. So the faithful in heaven are regarded as those who have been through the earthly battle and have served with honour.

## ASSIMILATION

Reviewing Old English poetry as a whole, the feature which stands out above all others is the apparently complete assimilation of the heroic and the Christian. The heroic code in Old English literature originated in the way the Germanic tribes organized themselves in the Migration Age in the warrior band. The ideal was unbending loyalty, unflinching bravery, even in the face of impossible odds. Dishonour lay in giving in, running away, coming to terms with enemies, and above all, transferring loyalty to anyone implicated in the death of one's lord.

All this can be seen to have been inherited by the Christian Anglo-Saxons and it is the basic background of the texts dealt with above. These all illustrate how Old English poetry merges and integrates the heroic and the Christian. What is abundantly clear is that the Anglo-Saxons who composed and wrote and copied these texts in no sense thought of the heroic code as heathen, even though they knew it had existed before they became Christian. For them it was the way things were, the way life normally was. In other words, their world view was heroic. To talk, as some scholars do, of the 'competing ideals' of Christianity and the heroic code in Anglo-Saxon England is a nonsense. The mode of Anglo-Saxon Christian verse is predominantly heroic, and as such it reflects the Christian culture from which it emerged.

# THE DREAM OF THE ROOD
## (TEXT 34)

One of the most remarkable and beautiful of Old English poems is The Dream of the Rood. It is a poem of 156 lines in a collection of religious verse and prose called the Vercelli Book. In it a man recounts a vision where he sees a beautiful tree covered in jewels. The tree tells a story full of pathos and wonder. And, as a kind of representative of the poem's audience, the dreamer responds to it.

There is much that is remarkable about the poem. There is the way the biblical story of the crucifixion is given a fresh and vivid telling. Or the way the poet uses the heroic conventions of Old English poetry to deal with deep theological issues. Any summary can only scratch the surface of the poet's art. But like any good story, the Dream catches our attention and engages our interest from the very beginning.

One of the arresting things is the way the poet creates a dreamlike quality in the opening lines. Initially, there is exotic beauty, bright light and geometric patterns. The tree in the air divides the world into quarters with jewels at the extremities. And clustering in the middle of the cross-beam are five jewels: these represent the five wounds of Christ, but we do not realize this yet. Angels of heaven, the saints, people on earth and the whole created order focuses intently on the glorious tree. The vision evokes nothing so strongly as what you might see lying down under the cupola, the great dome, of a Roman or Byzantine cathedral, and looking up: an unearthly sense of timeless proportion and infinite glory, with frescoes of crowds of angels and people all straining to see the cosmic drama.

But a note of disquiet creeps in. The poet assures us the tree in question is not the gallows of a criminal, and indeed he feels dirty in the presence of such purity as the tree of victory embodies. No, the tree is the tree of the Lord, adorned with gold and studded with gems. But again, in a terrifying shift such as occur without warning in dreams, the gold and gems melt away, and blood starts to ooze from the right side of the cross. Signs of earlier violence appear. The vision shimmers between unutterable beauty and stark terror, and the dreamer just lies there, unable to move and unable to take in what is happening. Then the cross speaks.

As the cross starts its story, it adopts the plaintive, weary tone of the victim. It was cut down, made into a gallows, set up on a hill, and made to crucify criminals. All this it wearily recounts; all this was done to it. But then, suddenly and without warning, the Lord of mankind appears, eager and active, wishing to climb up on the cross. This presents the cross with a dilemma. The adrenaline flows, and it considers the options, fight or flight. It throws off the mantle of the victim, responding directly to the commands of its lord. It has power now: it could kill its enemies, but it will not. It could flee, but it dare not.

The serene and confident young hero, God almighty himself, prepares for battle. He strips, as Germanic warriors did, and climbs up on the gallows, intent on saving his people. He is in control, self-determining, expressing his lordship. There is no compulsion. The cross trembles at the fearful embrace of its lord, yet it still stands firm. Together, they are mocked and abused. The wounds are still visible on the cross, it is still marked by the stains of the blood which flowed from the hero's side when he was pierced after he died. The light ebbs and drains away, and the brightness which the appearance of the Lord had brought is swallowed up, engulfed by cloud and shadow. It is as if the whole creation is mourning. Christ is on the cross. This single half-line is the turning-point and climax of the poem.

The cross once again becomes a passive observer after this flurry of activity. Loyal retainers come to take away the body of their lord, and they abandon the battle-wounded cross. The retainers carry the limp body, make a burial chamber, sing the dirge. And as once again the light ebbs with the onset of the evening, they leave their lord to rest. The crosses, fixed in the ground, weep as the voices fade and as the body grows cold in the tomb. In their turn, they too are taken down and buried. Yet, in due course, the Lord's retainers find out the whereabouts of the loyal cross, and adorn it with gold and silver.

In a strong and confident tone, the cross now explains its role and the reason for its conflicting appearances. It was once the most cruel of torments. But since the Son of God suffered on it, it has been transformed. It is now dignified and honoured, and towers over the earth in glory, just as the dreamer saw at the beginning of the vision. Its own story is an echo and a sidelight on the greatest story, the story of how almighty God suffered death for the sin of all people. The cross urges the dreamer to tell the vision, so that people will know and be prepared for the judgement when their Lord returns.

The dreamer is filled with joy as he understands the meaning of his vision. Even though he is lonely, he knows now that his friends have simply gone before him to the great banquet of heaven. And his mind is quickened with anticipation of the bliss and glory which will be his when he is brought by the cross into the presence of the Lord and his saints. They will all be joined by the souls of the righteous when, to complete the victory of the heroic Son of God, he returns from an expedition to hell with a great host of those who died before his historic sacrifice. At the beginning of the poem, angels and saints strained to see the unfolding drama of the Son of God's battle with death. The poem closes with angels and saints welcoming the victorious Son home from his expeditions with the spoils of war, the souls he has rescued. The poem begins with a vision of all creation gazing upon a single event in time. It closes with the completion of cosmic history, the eternal reign of the victorious Christ.

# INTERACTIONS OF HEROIC AND CHRISTIAN

There are all kinds of ways in which the poet uses the form and vocabulary of the heroic tradition to reinforce his theological meaning. The two enrich each other. In the cross's speech, lines 28–121, there are about twenty different expressions for Christ, several of which are repeated. This is the poet exploiting the rich vocabulary of honorific titles that Old English has built up. Many of these words or phrases proclaim Christ's deity, such as *god ælmihtig*, 'God almighty', *ric cyning*, 'powerful King', *heofena hlaford*, 'Lord of the Heavens'.

The number and variety of such expressions might lead us
to believe that they are used indiscriminately. But if we look
more closely we see this is not the case. In line 83, the cross
reports 'the Son of God suffered on me for a time'. This is the
only time the poet uses the term *beam godes*, 'Son of God'. It
has two close echoes in the crucifixion story: the mocking of
those who passed by, saying 'Come down from the cross if you
are the Son of God', and the comment of the centurion at
Jesus' death, 'Truly this was the Son of God'. Being the Son of
God meant suffering.

Then we might note the phrase used of Jesus in line 67,
*sigora wealdend*, 'the lord of victories'. Again, this kind of epithet is to be expected of a hero in secular verse, but here it
gains wonderful resonance from the fact that Christ is dead.
How can a dead man be *sigora wealdend*? Theologically, it was
by his death that Christ won salvation for humanity. This is
a powerful paradox, but the poet captures it beautifully in a
single phrase. The poet has formulated Christian doctrine in
heroic terms.

One of the words for Jesus that the poet uses only twice in
the poem is *Crist*. The lines from 50 to 55 get progressively
more breathless. There is also a change in narrative voice,
from the cross describing its experiences (I did this, I saw that)
to the simple statement of a universal truth, 'Christ was on the
cross'. This line, *crist wæs on rode*, is the emphatic focus of
the ever-shorter sentences in the passage. The line appears in
runes on the Ruthwell Cross, where it is similarly emphatic. Its
power lies in the utter simplicity and hammering effect of the
sequence of short words.

The words for death which are used reflect the poet's ability to frame theology in heroic terms. *Limwerig*, 'weary of
limb', *reste*, 'rested', *methe*, 'exhausted', are all words used as

euphemisms for death in the secular heroic poems. They try to cover up and protect the audience from the harsh reality, rather like our own phrases 'passed on', 'fell asleep' and so on. As heroic euphemisms, they would occur naturally in the context of a heroic death. But it is surely no accident that the poet uses words which suggest that death is not the end for this particular hero. He is weary after the great battle, but in a little while he will rise victorious from death. And as the conquering hero who plunders hell of its captives, he is *sigorfœst*, 'victorious', *mihtig and spedig*, 'mighty and successful'.

Then let us look at *mæte weorode*, 'with a small company'. When this phrase is used in the literature, it refers to a situation where a lord is vulnerable, because he does not have his full body of retainers with him. The poet of *The Dream of the Rood* uses this phrase in line 69 to mean, by understatement, completely alone, abandoned (as at line 124). Jesus in the tomb is alone, forsaken. But alongside this, we should note that in line 51 the poet refers to him as *weruda god*, 'the God of Hosts', a direct translation of the biblical phrase coming through the Vulgate as *dominus deus sabaoth*. Jesus could have called out twelve legions of angels. So here we have the Lord of Hosts, Almighty God, the Lord of Heaven, abandoned by his host, weak and ultimately alone in his death on earth. I doubt if the doctrine of *kenosis*, the self-emptying of Christ referred to in Philippians 2:7, has ever been more poetically captured.

# SOURCES

Much more could be said about the heroic and Christian elements of the poem. But it is perhaps more important to allow it to dispel any remaining illusions we might have as to the primitiveness of Anglo-Saxon poetry or Christianity. As we explore the poem further, an astonishing wealth of sources and influences comes to light. *The Dream of the Rood* is an extraordinarily learned poem. At the most obvious level we have the adaptation of ancient snatches of runic verse from the Ruthwell Cross into a longer narrative and theological poem (Text 35). The poem as we have it in the Vercelli Book dates from the end of the tenth century, and it was written out in the south of England. The cross of Ruthwell, in Dumfries, Scotland, was probably carved in the eighth century. The two versions of the poem of the cross are separated by hundreds of miles and hundreds of years. They are united by artistic genius and love of the tradition and story of salvation.

Among the main sources are of course the gospels, and the poem keeps fairly closely to the central narrative. The poet uses key details from the gospels: the crucifixion place being a hill, the darkness which fell in the early afternoon, the nailing and mocking. The poet uses the phrase *gast onsended*, 'he gave up his spirit', an exact translation of *emisit spiritum* of Matthew 27:50. What is most striking is the way the poet incorporates details from the different gospels: in lines 36–7, the reference to the shaking of the earth seems likely to be the earthquake mentioned only in Matthew. The mention of the cross bleeding from the right hand side in line 20 is probably a reference to the spear thrust into Christ's side, mentioned only in John's gospel. Likewise the warriors who take Christ down from the cross and put him in the tomb must also be a reference to John's gospel where Joseph of Arimathea is helped by Nicodemus in doing this, whereas in the other gospels only Joseph is mentioned. This suggests a sensitivity to the variety of the biblical sources.

Then there is a wide range of references to other Christian sources. Lines 101 onwards are a remarkably accurate rendition of the Apostles' Creed. Christ suffered, died and was buried, rose again, ascended and will come again to judge. The omission of the descent to the dead is interesting at this point, because the poem ends with it, expanded into the medieval Christian commonplace known as the Harrowing of Hell. There is a similar set piece on the Judgement Day in lines 110 onwards, another homiletic commonplace.

The image of the cross as *beacen*, 'sign, symbol, standard', is one familiar from Latin hymns, where the cross is the *vexillum*, 'battle standard' of the king. This is a reference to the famous late sixth-century hymn *Vexilla Regis* by Venantius Fortunatus. Fortunatus was Bishop of Poitiers in the south of France until his death in 609, and one of the greatest hymn-writers of the early Middle Ages. Another of his hymns features in the poem, the one still popular today in J. M. Neale's translation as 'Sing my tongue the glorious battle'. The idea of the cross as a loyal retainer is one which is anticipated by the phrase *crux fidelis*, 'faithful cross' in Fortunatus's hymn. And similarly, *signum triumphale*, 'victory sign', finds an echo in *sigebeam*, 'tree of victory' in line 14.

More widely still, the poem engages constructively in the contemporary debates of the Church. The early medieval church was obsessed with christology. Christology has to do with the nature and work of Christ, and obviously it was an important topic. Debates and splits in the church were rife as one theory was proposed and adopted by one church council, and overturned at the next. The main debate in the Anglo-Saxon period was to do with whether Jesus had one nature or two: whether he was both divine *and* human (as the Council of Chalcedon in AD 451 said), or just one *or* the other (as two broad groups called Monophysites said). The focus of these debates was the crucifixion. If Jesus suffered, the Monophysites argued, he could not be God, because God cannot suffer.

In this context of heated and often acrimonious controversy, the poet coolly and carefully depicts his Lord. He avoids
putting too much stress on the humanity and suffering of Jesus
by representing him as an ideal warrior, the divine king, nobly
and voluntarily undertaking battle. Much of the suffering is
experienced through the cross, rather than directly by the
heroic Christ. But at the same time the poet does not under-
state the suffering and pain of the crucifixion, since the cross is
not only covered in blood, but also is represented as feeling the
agony. Like a true hero, the Christ of the poem makes little of
his suffering in the great battle. But no Anglo-Saxon would
mistake bravery for inability to feel pain.

Other controversies are treated with similar grace and skill
in the poem. The growth of the cult of the cross in Anglo-
Saxon England, perhaps at the expense of the cult of the
Virgin Mary, is referred to in lines 90–94, where the comparison between them is made. Similarly, a long-standing argument about the value of pilgrimage is obliquely referred to in
line 118, where St Jerome's statement that going to visit holy
sites is not as important as bearing the cross in your heart is
echoed. I think it is likely that the poet had been on pilgrimage, and that the opening scene of the poem reflects his recol-
lection of the grandeur of a Roman basilica. But he knows that
such things are not central to faith, whereas the cross is.

All these things point to a phenomenally literate poet or
succession of poets, who drew on a wide range of Christian
sources, and assimilated them beautifully to the Anglo-Saxon
cultural context. Perhaps just as remarkable is the fact that the
poet still has a considerable degree of freedom. The sources do
not constrict the poet. There is the imaginative device of the
cross telling the story. This is probably borrowed from Anglo-
Saxon riddling technique, where the object often describes

itself before asking the listener to say what it is. And at lines 65 onwards, the actions of Jesus' retainers at the burial are particularly Germanic. Jesus is taken down from the cross and the warriors stand by his head, then make him a *moldærn*, 'an earth-hall' or burial chamber, made out of bright stone. Then they sing a dirge before leaving. This in its broad outline was the normal way to conduct a hero's funeral in Anglo-Saxon England. Beowulf's funeral is substantially similar (Text 33). None of it is in the gospels: Jesus' body is given to Joseph of Arimathea, who lays it in his own tomb and has a stone put across the entrance. So the poet is using his imagination to naturalize the Christian tradition.

## THE WAY OF THE CROSS

*The Dream of the Rood* is one of the most significant monuments of Old English poetry. It is neither pure theology nor pure imagination, but a creative blend of the two, faithful to both. It has the astonishing effect it has because it uses heroic and Christian elements together to give fresh impact to 'the greatest story ever told'. The poem has a place within a definite tradition, a tradition which embraces the different kinds of poems we looked at earlier. But it transcends that tradition. All the things we find strange about the cult of the cross and the debates on christology are insignificant because the poem enables us to see the crucifixion with new eyes.

The poem captures both the pathos and the joy of the Anglo-Saxons' experience of their faith and their understanding of the cross. And it allows us to enter into that experience by awakening our imagination with something fresh and vivid and delightful. The way of the cross for them was the way of heroic loyalty, obedience, and suffering. It involved study and thought, doctrine and orthodoxy, art and imagination. It was a complete, unified way of life, lived intimately with God, lived faithfully in the world. The fragmented modern world, both secular and religious, has a lot to learn from it.

# CONCLUSION

In this book we have tried to let Anglo-Saxon Christianity speak for itself. We have listened to the stories and have responded to the texts. We have also asked questions of the Anglo-Saxons, because we want to understand what they are saying to us. Three things have emerged most clearly as characteristic of Anglo-Saxon Christianity.

Firstly, Anglo-Saxon Christianity is characterized by *engagement*. It was not a spectator faith, or an elaborate game. It shaped the culture, it created new ways of thinking, it opposed some old ways of thinking. It was realistic and holistic, seeing all of life as the sphere of God's interest and action. The Anglo-Saxons enjoyed the humour of St Gregory's punning in the market-place, probably as much as the rude riddler's punning in the Exeter Book. And they felt the vulnerability of human life like a sparrow flying nervously through a hall and out into the storm and darkness. Anglo-Saxon Christianity engaged with the past, the present and the future. Abraham's defence of Sodom before God in Genesis 18 was heroic: 'Far be it from you to do such a thing – to kill the righteous with the wicked! ... What if ten righteous can be found there?' The Anglo-Saxon poet of *Beowulf* asked the same question of his ancestors: what of the righteous heathen? Past and present mattered.

Secondly, Anglo-Saxon Christianity is characterized by *pragmatism*. It recognized that life does not stand still, and faith is exercised in the decisions and choices that have to be made. Pope Gregory's pragmatism about working with people's habits in the matter of religion enabled the Christian faith to supplant heathenism quickly and without bloodshed. The debates over the date of the celebration of Easter will hardly strike us as quite matching the festival in holiness. But even if the Anglo-Saxons got some things in it wrong, the decision itself made significant progress possible. Anglo-Saxon Christianity recognized the value of expressing the faith in familiar terms, like those of the heroic code of the warrior culture. Jesus' parables described the kingdom of God in terms of ordinary things. But there were limits, and if a Psalm was so passionate about vengeance that it recommended atrocity, then the Anglo-Saxon poet could revise it.

Thirdly, Anglo-Saxon Christianity is characterized by *integrity*. The art and literature of the Anglo-Saxons is patterned, and this patterning reflects their life. It has regularity, but it is not mechanical. It has variety and exuberance, but it is not chaotic. Anglo-Saxon Christianity understood God to be a God of order, so monastic life was disciplined, following a regular pattern of worship and service. There was no separation of faith and works, but a sensitive response to the needs and abilities of the individual within a pattern of corporate life. Bede could spend his time for labour at work in the library, and it was regarded as work just as much as the smith sweating over his anvil. It was integrity that enabled the Anglo-Saxons to respond to miracle stories in a calm and thoughtful way: God works in mysterious ways, but reveals those ways through the patterns and paradigms of scripture.

Western people today often live disengaged lives. Because science has replaced religion as the system which explains everything, faith has ceased to engage with the problems and issues of life, and has become a purely personal ethic. People have become so afraid of offending others, at the political and social level as much as the religious, that they rarely do anything. People live lives of such bewildering complexity or monotonous repetitiveness, that life ceases to reflect the enriching pattern of God's variety. It has become hard to care, hard to see what you can do, and hard to claim that faith is an integrating factor in life. Intellect and faith hardly ever inter-act, work reflects only technology, not art, and value for the individual comes only from what he or she does, not is. In its engagement, pragmatism and integrity, and in many other ways, Anglo-Saxon Christianity has much to teach.

ANGLO-SAXON CHRISTIANITY

# TEXTS

The Anglo-Saxon and other texts translated here are generally those that are too long to fit neatly into the discussion in the chapters. They are not all equally important. Some are here because I blush to include them in the main text!

**Text 1**: An account of Pope Gregory's visit to the market.

Among the other goods, Gregory saw some boys for sale with pale skin, beautiful hair and handsome faces. It is reported that when he saw them, he asked where they had been brought from. He was told they were from the island of Britain, where the people looked like that. His next question was whether the people of that island were Christians or still tied up in heathen error. He was told they were heathen. Heaving a long sigh, he said, 'How sad that the lord of darkness should have people so bright-faced. And that grace should appear in the countenance when no grace is present in the mind.' He asked further what the name of the people was, and was told they were called Angles. 'Good,' he said, 'because they have the faces of angels, and such people must inherit heaven with the angels. What is the name of the province they have been brought from?' He was told that the inhabitants of the province were called Deirans. 'Good,' he said, 'they will be plucked out of the wrath (*de ira*) of Christ and called to his mercy. And what is the king of this province called?' 'Ælle,' he was told. 'Alleluia!,' he said, playing on the name. 'They must sing the praise of God the Creator in those parts!'

So he went to the Pope of Rome, the apostolic see, and asked for preachers of the word to be sent to the Angles of Britain to convert them to Christ.

From Bede's Latin, *Ecclesiastical History*, book 2, chapter 1.

Text 2: Augustine of Canterbury's fears.

About one hundred and fifty years after the arrival of the Angles in Britain, [Pope] Gregory sent the servant of God, Augustine, and a number of other God-fearing monks with him, to preach the word of God to the English people. They undertook this work in obedience to the pope's orders, and had gone some distance on the journey when they were paralysed with fear and began to think about returning home rather than going to a barbarous, savage, and unbelieving people, whose language they did not know. All of them agreed that this was the safer course. So they sent Augustine back straight away ... humbly to ask from St Gregory permission to give up such a dangerous, difficult and uncertain venture. But Gregory sent them an encouraging letter ...

From Bede's Latin, *Ecclesiastical History*, book 1, chapter 23. Bede had the papal archives in Rome searched for material relating to the conversion of the Anglo-Saxons. It is possible that the reference to the 'barbarous, savage, and unbelieving people' is actually quoted from the letter. It shows the fine Roman disdain and fear of the 'barbarians'. And it shows that Bede could laugh at himself.

**Text 3:** Augustine's encounter with King Æthelberht of Kent.

[The king has let the monks land on Thanet, and has received an initial message from them.] After a few days, the king came to the island. Sitting in the open air, he ordered Augustine and his companions to him, to talk. He was cautious not to meet them in a building, for according to ancient superstition, he believed that if they possessed any magical powers they might be able to deceive and overpower him. But they came to him not with demonic, but with divine power, carrying as their battle-standard a silver cross and the image of the Lord and Saviour painted on a panel. And they sang litanies asking the Lord for the eternal salvation of themselves and those to whom they came.

At the king's order, they sat down and preached the word of life to the king and all the retainers with him. In response the king said, 'The words and promises you bring are fair. But they are new and untried, and I cannot just accept them and abandon the beliefs that the whole English nation has held to for so long. You have travelled a long way, though, and I can see that you want to tell us those things which you believe to be true and very good. So we will not trouble you, but will receive you with hospitality and will make it our business to provide the things you need. Nor will we prohibit you from preaching and winning to your faith all you can.'

From Bede's Latin, *Ecclesiastical History*, book 1, chapter 25.

**Text 4:** The life of the monks at Canterbury.

As soon as they had established themselves in the house given them [by King Æthelberht], they began to emulate the life of the apostles and the early church. They spent their time in constant prayers, vigils and fasting, preaching the word of life to everyone they could. They despised all goods of this world as unnecessary, and accepted only vital necessities from those they taught. They practised everything they taught in their lives, and were prepared patiently to suffer and even to die for the truth that they preached.

From Bede's Latin, *Ecclesiastical History*, book 1, chapter 26.

**Text 5:** One of Pope Gregory's letters to Augustine, warning him not to be elated by miracles.

My dearly loved brother,
I know that almighty God, for love of you, has worked great marvels for the people that he wished to call his elect. It is necessary that you should have both fearful joy and joyful fear over this heavenly gift. Rejoice that the souls of the English are attracted by the outward wonders to inward grace. Fear that in the process of

working these signs, the unsteady soul may elevate itself presumptuously, and that which raises it to outward honour may be the cause of its fall into vainglory ... Not all the elect work wonders, but their names are all written in heaven ... Whatever powers of working signs you have received, or will receive, they are not given to you, but through you for the salvation of others.

From Bede's Latin, *Ecclesiastical History*, book 1, chapter 31. An interesting sidelight on this rather stern warning comes from a *Life* of St Gregory written by a monk of Whitby, probably sometime near the end of the seventh century. The monk complains that his sources for Gregory's *Life* contain very few miracle stories. It appears that Gregory had a saner view of miracles than most of his contemporaries, or perhaps his gifts lay elsewhere than miracle-working.

**Text 6:** Pope Gregory's letter to Abbot Mellitus.

When almighty God has brought you to our most reverend brother Bishop Augustine, tell him what I have decided after careful thought about the English people. That is, that the idol temples of that nation should on no account be destroyed, but only the idols in them. Sprinkle holy water in those shrines, set up altars and place relics in them. For if the temples are well built, it is proper that they should be changed from the worship of devils to the service of the true God. So, when the people see that their temples are not destroyed they may be able to put away error from their hearts. And they will come to recognize and worship the true God in the places they are familiar with.

And since they are accustomed to slaughtering many
cattle as sacrifices to devils, some solemnity ought to
be substituted for them. So on the day of a dedication
or the festivals of the holy martyrs, whose relics are
kept there, have them construct booths for themselves
from the branches of trees around the churches which
have been converted out of shrines, and have them
celebrate the solemnity with religious feasting. They
should sacrifice animals to the devil no longer, but
should slaughter animals for food to the praise of God,
and give thanks to the Giver of all things for His plentiful provision. In this way, if some outward pleasures
are kept, the people will more readily desire inward,
spiritual pleasures.

From Bede's Latin, *Ecclesiastical History*, book 1, chapter 30.

## Text 7: The 'golden word of God'.

Solomon said,
'Golden is the word of God, studded with gems,
it has silver leaves and each one is able
65  separately to declare the gospel by the Spirit's power.
It is wisdom to the mind, honey to the soul,
and milk of the spirit, the most blessed of all famous
deeds.
It is able to bring the soul out of perpetual darkness
under the earth, though the fiend has fastened it
never so
70  deeply with fetters. Though he might lock it
with fifty bars, the golden word will break that device
and slice through the cunning contrivance.

It destroys hunger, despoils hell,
scatters billowing flame, builds up glory.
75    It is stronger on the earth,
more firmly fixed than the fixity of all stones.
To the lame, it is a doctor; light to the blinking;
an opening [of ears] to the deaf, tongue to the dumb,
a protection from the criminal ...

From the Old English *Solomon and Saturn*, I, *Anglo-Saxon Minor Poems*. The poem goes on for nearly another hundred lines describing the power and virtues of the Lord's Prayer, and the runic characters which make up parts of the first words. Interestingly, one of the more consistent images is of the letters as warriors, scattering and destroying enemies.

**Text 8:** *The Nine Herbs Charm.*
[The charmer invokes the power of the herbs by addressing them directly, then sums up:]

30    These nine are powerful against nine poisons.
A snake came writhing, and it bit a man.
Then Woden took nine glory-twigs,
and struck the serpent so that it fell into nine parts.
There apple and poison brought it about
35    that she never would live in the house [together].
Chervil and fennel, the very powerful pair,
[are] the herbs the wise Lord created
holy in the heavens, when he hung.
He made and sent them into the seven worlds,
40    to wretched and happy, a remedy for all.
This one keeps off pain, this attacks poison,
this is powerful against three and against thirty,
against enchantment of evil beings.

From the Old English, *The Nine Herbs Charm*, *Anglo-Saxon Minor Poems*. And so it goes on to list the colours of poison and the skin diseases the charm will protect against. The charm collects together anything that smacks of power and knowledge: lists, numbers, strange stories. And it fudges distinctions: 'the Lord' in line 37 could just as well be Woden as Christ – a Norse poem records Woden hanging himself to get occult knowledge. But Christ's power over all diseases is asserted in line 58, before the charmer claims special power for him or herself.

**Text 9:** More recipes.

> For dropsy, take dry dog's excrement and make it into a drink; it cures one suffering from dropsy.
>
> To drive out fever: give the ill person white dog's excrement ground to powder and mixed with flour, baked into a small cake, to eat. Give it to him, day or night, before the fever approaches; the fit will be severe, but afterwards it will diminish and go away.
>
> For dropsy, take dog's vomit and bind it on the abdomen; the dropsy flows out with the liquid.

From the Old English *Medicina de Quadrupedibus*. The word translated 'fever' also means 'dwarf', and it may be that some idea of oppression by malicious spirits is present, even in this learned translation of a classical work. Don't try this at home.

**Text 10:** A miracle contest.

> With the help of King Æthelberht, Augustine called together the bishops and teachers of the nearby British

provinces for a conference at a place still called Augustine's Oak, which is on the border of the Hwicce and the East Saxons. And he began to urge them with brotherly advice, that in catholic peace they should take joint responsibility with him for the evangelizing of the heathen for the Lord's sake. They did not keep Easter at the right time, but between the fourteenth and the twentieth day of the lunar month, which calculation is based on a cycle of 84 years. They did many other things in which they ran counter to the unity of the church. After a long discussion they were unwilling to agree, despite the prayers, advice and rebukes of Augustine. They preferred their own traditions to those which all the churches throughout the world agree on in Christ. The holy father Augustine brought the long and tedious process to a close by saying, 'Let us plead with God, "who makes people of one mind" in his Father's house, that he might show us by some heavenly signs which tradition is to be followed ... Bring some sick person in, and let the faith and practice of the one by whom he is healed be accepted as pleasing to God, and right for all to follow.' His adversaries agreed reluctantly, and a blind English person was brought in, and was presented to the British bishops, but gained no cure or benefit from their ministry. Then Augustine, driven on by necessity, fell on his knees before the Father of our Lord Jesus Christ, praying that he would restore the man's lost sight, and by that enlightenment of the body of one man, would bring the light of spiritual grace to the hearts of many believers. Immediately the blind man's sight returned, and everyone acknowledged Augustine as the true preacher of the light of heaven. Then the Britons said they understood that Augustine preached the true way of righteousness, but that they could not abandon their old customs without the agreement of their own people. So they asked that another synod should be held, and more should come to it.

From Bede's Latin, *Ecclesiastical History*, book 2, chapter 2. Here, and often elsewhere, Bede specifies the dreadful heresy into which the British had fallen, calculating Easter 'between the fourteenth and the twentieth day of the lunar month ... on a cycle of 84 years'.

**Text 11:** King Edwin's council.
Coifi, the chief priest of the heathen religion, speaks.

'O king, consider this matter which is now being preached to us. I tell you truly that, as far as I can learn, the religion which we have hitherto professed has neither power nor profit in it. None of your people has devoted himself more diligently to the worship of our gods than I have, and yet there are many who receive greater benefits and greater honour from you than I do and are more prosperous in all the things they do. If the gods had any power they would have favoured me more, as I have always made it my business to serve them with greater zeal. Therefore it remains to be said that if on examination these new things which have now been preached to us are better and more effectual, we should accept them without any delay.'

Another of the king's chief men agreed with this argument and with these wise words and then added,

'It appears to me, O king, that the present life of man on earth, in comparison with that time which is unknown to us, is like this. You are sitting at the feast with your noblemen and warriors in wintertime. A good fire is burning on the hearth in the middle of the hall and all inside is warm, while outside the winter storms of rain and snow are raging. A sparrow flies swiftly through the hall. It comes in at one door and quickly flies out through the other. For the time it is inside, the storm and wintry tempest cannot touch it, but after the briefest moment of quiet, it vanishes from your sight. It flies out of the winter storm and quickly into it again. So this human life appears for a short time: of what is to follow, and what went before, we are completely ignorant. So if this new doctrine gives us more certain information, it seems right that we should follow it.' Other elders and counsellors of the king said the same things by divine prompting.

Coifi added that he wished to listen still more carefully to what Paulinus himself preached about God, and when Paulinus had done that at the king's command, Coifi exclaimed, 'I have long since realized that there is nothing in our religion. For the more earnestly I sought the truth in our cult, the less I found it. Now I publicly confess that in this preaching the truth clearly shines out which can confer on us the gifts of life, salvation, and eternal happiness. Therefore I advise your majesty that we should instantly abandon and burn down the temples and the altars we have consecrated to no advantage.' Why need I say more? The king publicly allowed Paulinus to preach the gospel, and renouncing idolatry, professed faith in Christ. When he enquired of their high priest who should be the first to desecrate the altars and shrines of the idols, together with the surrounding enclosures, Coifi answered, 'I will. For who more properly can destroy those things which I foolishly worshipped and so set an example to all? Who more properly than myself, now that God has given me true wisdom?' And immediately, despising his vain superstitions, he asked the king to give him weapons and a stallion. And mounting the horse, he set out to destroy the idols. It was not allowed for a high priest of their religion to carry weapons or to ride on anything but a mare. So with a sword belted round his waist and carrying a spear in his hand, he mounted the king's stallion and set off to where the idols were. The ordinary people who saw him thought he was mad. But without hesitation, as soon as he reached the shrine he desecrated it by throwing into it the spear which he carried. And rejoicing greatly in the knowledge of the worship of the true God, he ordered his companions to destroy and burn down the shrine and all the enclosures. The place where the idols were is still shown, not far east from York, beyond the River Derwent. It is called Goodmanham today, where the high priest, by the inspiration of the true God, desecrated and destroyed the altars which he himself had consecrated.

From Bede's Latin, *Ecclesiastical History*, book 2, chapter 13.

**Text 12:** The Germanic tribes described by Tacitus.

There is great rivalry, both among the followers to obtain the highest place in their leader's estimation and among the chiefs for the honour of having the biggest and most valiant retinue. Both prestige and power depend on being continually attended by a large train of picked young warriors, which is a distinction in peace and protection in war ...

On the field of battle it is a disgrace to a chief to be surpassed in courage by his followers, and to the followers not to equal the courage of their chief. And to leave a battle alive after their chief has fallen means lifelong infamy and shame. To defend and protect him, and to let him get the credit for their own acts of heroism, are the most solemn obligations of their allegiance. The chiefs fight for victory, the followers for their chief. Many noble youths, if the land of their birth is stagnating in a long period of peace and inactivity, deliberately seek out other tribes which have some war in hand. For the Germans have no taste for peace; renown is more easily won among perils, and a large body of retainers cannot be kept together except by means of violence and war. They are always making demands on the generosity of their chief, asking for a coveted war-horse or a spear stained with the blood of a defeated enemy. Their meals, for which plentiful if homely fare is provided, count in lieu of pay. The wherewithal for this openhandedness comes from war and plunder.

From Tacitus' Latin, *Germania*, chapters 13 and 14, in the translation of H. Mattingly.

**Text 13:** Gildas on the Anglo-Saxon invasion.

Then all the councillors, together with that proud tyrant [Vortigern], the British king, were so blinded, that, as a protection to their country, they sealed its doom by inviting in among them (like wolves into the sheep-fold), the fierce and impious Saxons, a race hateful both to God and men, to repel the invasions of the northern nations. What palpable darkness must have enveloped their minds – darkness desperate and cruel! ...

A multitude of whelps came forth from the lair of this barbaric lioness, in three cyuls, as they call them, that is in three ships of war ... They first landed on the eastern side of the island, by the invitation of the unlucky king, and there they fixed their sharp talons, apparently to fight in favour of the island, but alas! more truly against it. Their mother-land, finding her first brood thus successful, sends forth a larger company of her wolfish offspring, which sailing over, join themselves to their bastard-born comrades ... The barbarians being thus introduced as soldiers into the island, to encounter, as they falsely said, any dangers in defence of their hospitable entertainers, obtain an allowance of provisions, which, for some time being plentifully bestowed, stopped their doggish mouths. Yet they complain that their monthly supplies are not furnished in sufficient abundance, and they industriously aggravate each occasion of a quarrel, saying that unless more liberality is shown them, they will break the treaty and plunder the whole island. In a short time they follow up their threats with deeds ...

All the columns were levelled with the ground by the frequent strokes of the battering-ram, all the husbandmen routed, together with their bishops, priests, and people, whilst the sword gleamed, and the flames crackled around them on every side. Lamentable to behold, in the midst of the streets lay the tops of lofty towers, tumbled to the ground, stones of high walls, holy altars, fragments of human bodies, covered with livid clots of coagulated blood, looking as if they had been squeezed together in a press ...

From the Latin of Gildas, *The Ruin of Britain*, sections 23–4, in the translation of J. A. Giles.

**Text 14:** Byrhtnoth the soldier of Christ.

The warrior [Byrhtnoth] became enraged; he stabbed
   with his spear
the proud viking who had wounded him.
140 The warrior was experienced: he had his spear pass
through the young man's neck, his hand guided it
so that he took the life from the sudden attacker.
Then he quickly pierced another,
   so that his mailshirt fell apart: that one was wounded
   in the chest
145 through the locked rings, and the deadly point
   was fixed in his heart. The nobleman was all the more
   cheerful.
He laughed, then, the bold man, and gave thanks
   to God
for the day's work that the Lord had given him.

Byrhtnoth is wounded by a viking, and falls to the ground.

He looked up towards heaven:
'Thank you, Lord of the nations,
for all the joys that I have experienced on earth.
175 Now, kind Lord, my greatest need is that
you grant grace to my spirit,
that my soul might be allowed to journey to you,
travel in peace into your control,
Lord of the angels. I beseech you
180 that hellish attackers may not be allowed to harm it.'
Then heathen men hacked him to pieces,
and both the warriors who stood beside him.

From the Old English poem, *The Battle of Maldon*. See also
Text 16 below for a different attitude, but one that the Anglo-
Saxons would have appreciated equally.

**Text 15:** Bede's concern about false monasteries.

Though it is shameful to speak of it, such people have
made so many places to pass under the name of monasteries, when they themselves are utterly lacking in the
monastic life (as you know well), that there is no place
where the sons of the nobility or retired warriors can be
given possessions of their own.

From Bede's Latin, *Letter to Ecgberht*, section 11.

**Text 16:** The martyrdom of King Edmund.

[The Danish army] travelled far and wide through the
land, harrying and killing, as their habit is. The most
important leaders of the sailors were Hinguar and

Hubba, united through the devil. They landed with their ships in Northumbria, and laid waste the land and killed the people. Then, having won victory through savagery, Hinguar turned east with his ships, and left Hubba in Northumbria. Hinguar arrived by rowing among the East Anglians in the year that Prince Alfred, who later became famous as the king of the West Saxons, was twenty-one. And the aforementioned Hinguar suddenly crept like a wolf upon the land, and struck the people, men, women and innocent children, and shamefully oppressed the innocent Christians.

The Danes send a messenger to King Edmund demanding money with menaces. The king discusses the matter with a bishop, who suggests giving them what they want. Edmund disagrees.

After these words, Edmund turned to the messenger that Hinguar had sent, and boldly said, 'Truly you deserve death now, but I do not wish to sully my clean hands with your filthy blood. For I follow Christ who gave us an example in this. I will gladly be slain by you if that is what God ordains. Go now, with all speed, and tell your cruel lord, "Never will Edmund, alive, submit to Hinguar the savage general, unless he, Hinguar, first submits in faith to the Saviour Christ in this land."'

The messenger went quickly away, and on the road he met the savage Hinguar hurrying towards Edmund with all his army. And he told the wicked man how he was answered. Hinguar then arrogantly commanded his vikings to look out especially for the king who had rejected his offer, and immediately bind him.

So King Edmund stood in his hall when Hinguar came, and mindful of the Saviour, threw down his weapons. He wished to follow Christ's example, who forbade Peter to fight with weapons against the savage Jews. So the wicked men bound Edmund and abused him insultingly, and beat him with rods, and afterwards took the faithful king to a firmly rooted tree, and tied him to it with strong ropes, and then scourged him for a long time with whips. Between strokes, he kept calling out in true faith to the Saviour Christ. Because of his faith, and because he kept calling for help to Christ, the heathens became madly enraged. They shot at him, for their amusement, until he was covered with their missiles like the bristles on a hedgehog, just as St Sebastian was. Hinguar the wicked sailor saw that the noble king had no intention of renouncing Christ, but kept calling out to him with resolute faith. So he ordered him to be beheaded, and the heathen did it.

From the Old English, Ælfric's *Lives of the Saints*. Edmund died in 869, and a Latin *Life* was written about him by Abbo of Fleury, a monk who visited from France. Abbo heard the story from the mouth of St Dunstan, the great archbishop of Canterbury, when Abbo visited him in 985. Ælfric translated Abbo's *Life* at the end of the tenth century. This extract is just the beginning, the more historical part, of the story of the miracles of St Edmund. After his death, Edmund's sanctity is revealed by many things, including the decapitated head calling out to enable people to find it. Edmund was unusual in being venerated very early after his death, within thirty years

ANGLO-SAXON CHRISTIANITY

or so. A great hoard of silver was buried in 903 at Cuerdale in Cumbria and around 1,800 of the coins were minted in memory of St Edmund. Even the vikings honoured him.

**Text 17:** An 'adjusted' Psalm.
Compare the verses in the New International Version:

> Remember, O Lord, what the Edomites did on the day Jerusalem fell.
> 'Tear it down,' they cried, 'tear it down to its foundations!'
> O Daughter of Babylon, doomed to destruction,
> happy is he who repays you for what you have done to us –
> he who seizes your infants and dashes them against the rocks.

7.  Remember, Lord, the many children,
     all living, that are in Edom,
     when you enrich Jerusalem;
     those now often say, 'Let us make them destitute,
     until they choose their land.'

8.  Lo, you are Babylon's, her wretched daughter,
     bitterly, sadly and miserably afflicted!
     Yet blessed is he who pays back
     those [things] you ever granted him earlier,
     and that you also gave to us all.

9.  Blessed is he who takes and sets
     his own son on that noble rock.

From the Old English, Psalm 136 (= NIV 137). There are parts of this that are difficult to understand, and which probably mask the poet's own groping for the meaning of the Latin original. But the last verse is simple and clear in the Latin. There was no possibility of the poet misunderstanding it. The fact that his version of verse 9 is so close to the biblical verse, yet so far from it in intention, is clear evidence that he understood it perfectly, but changed it.

**Text 18: Ælfric's worries about translating the Bible.**

> Now it seems to me that this work is very dangerous for me or anyone else to undertake, because I fear that if some foolish man reads it or hears it read, he will think that he is allowed to live now in the new dispensation as the patriarchs lived before the old law was established, or how people lived under the law of Moses. Once I knew a certain priest, who was my schoolmaster at the time, and he had the book of Genesis, and knew a certain amount of Latin. He said of the patriarch Jacob that he had four wives – two sisters and their two maidservants. It was true what he said, but he did not know, nor I either at that point, how great is the division between the old law and the new. In the beginning of the world, brother had sister as wife, and sometimes even father bred with his own daughter, and many had more than one wife for the increase of the population, and in the early days people could only marry their own close family. If anyone wishes to live in this fashion now, since the coming of Christ, as people lived then before or under the law of Moses, that person is no Christian, and he does not deserve to have any Christian eat with him.

From the Old English, Ælfric's *Preface to Genesis*.

**Text 19:** On loneliness.

> The friendless unfortunate man will take wolves as
>     companions
> those highly dangerous animals. Very often these
>     companions tear him ...
>
> Wretched is the man who has to live alone –
> to dwell friendless is his lot.
> It would be better for him to have a brother,
> both of them the sons of one man, if they should have
>     to tackle a boar
> or tangle with a bear.

From the Old English, *Maxims I* in the Exeter Book. These two passages are quite widely separated in the poem, but both instinctively see isolation as being dangerous or sub-human.

**Text 20:** Alcuin on temptations monks fall prey to.

> Let us prepare ourselves for meeting the great king, so that we may find him kindly, for no one can escape him. Let us think daily what gift we will bring, as scripture says, 'Thou shalt not appear before the Lord God empty-handed'. No precious metal, no bright jewels, no vain clothing, no worldly luxury will be acceptable there to that fairest of Judges: only generosity of almsgiving, and multiplied good deeds will avail ...
>
> The words of God should be read at the monks' feasts. There the reader should be heard not a harpist, the discourses of the Fathers not the songs of the heathens. What has Ingeld to do with Christ? The house is

narrow, it cannot contain both. The king of the heavens will have nothing to do with heathen and damned so-called kings. For the eternal king rules in the heavens, the lost heathen repines in hell. The voices of readers should be heard in your houses, not the cackling of the crowd in the street.

From Alcuin's Latin, *Letter 124*. Written to Higbald of Lindisfarne in 797. The accusation levelled at Lindisfarne, that they indulged in gaudy dress and had personal possessions as well as listening to popular tales, reflects Alcuin's fear that a slackening of standards invites God's judgement.

**Text 21:** Alcuin's interpretation of numbers.

Be obedient to his will, according to the name Simon, who for the feast of the Lord pulled in the net, full of large fish, 153 of them. If you wish to know what these fish are which are defined in this number, they are the ones chosen for the perpetual banquet with Christ after the final resurrection, by means of the Ten Commandments and seven-fold gifts of the Spirit ... If you add each individual number from one to seventeen one after the other, the total comes to 153. If you split seventeen into two parts, ten and seven, ten denotes the Commandments, and seven the gifts of the Spirit. Likewise, if you split seven into two, into three and four that is, three stands for faith in the Holy Trinity, the faith by which all nations are to be saved, and these [faithful ones] are spread to the four corners of the entire world.

From Alcuin's Latin, *Letter 113*.

**Text 22:** A woman's song.

I recite this song about myself, miserable,
and about my fate. I can say what miseries
I have endured since I grew up,
recently and long ago, but never more than now.
5   I have always suffered torment from my miseries.
        First my lord went away from his people
over the tumult of the waves. I had anxious mornings
over where in the world my chieftain was.
When I went to find a retinue,
10  a friendless exile, because of my dire need,
the man's kinsmen began plotting,
with dark intent, to separate us
so that we two have lived as far apart in the world
    as can be,
and have lived most miserably – and I have suffered
    longing.
15  My lord commanded me to make my home here.
I had no loved one, no loyal friends
in this place, and so my heart is sad.
Then I found the man close to my heart
dogged by misfortune, miserable,
20  uncommunicative and bloody-minded.
With cheerful demeanour we so often vowed
that nothing would separate us, nothing at all,
but death alone. That is all changed.
Our love is now as if
25  it had never been. I must suffer, near and far,
the feud of my dearly loved one.

> I was told to live in a forest grove
> under an oak-tree in that earth-cave.
> The cave is old, I am overcome with longing,
> 30  the valleys are dim, the hills mountainous,
> the enclosing hedges sharp, overgrown with brambles –
> a joyless place. The departure of my lord
> often wracks me with pain here. There are lovers on earth
> living in love, sharing the bed,
> 35  when I at daybreak walk alone
> round this earth-cave under the oak-tree.
> I have to sit there for the days long as summer:
> there I can weep over my miseries,
> my many sufferings – because I cannot ever
> 40  rest from my sorrow,
> nor from all the longing that has come upon me in
>         this life ...
> 50      My friend, he too suffers
> great misery. He remembers all too frequently
> a more joyful dwelling. Woe it is for one who must
> wait with longing for a loved one.

From the Old English, *The Wife's Lament*, in the Exeter Book.

**Text 23:** Another woman's song.

> It is with my people as if they are given a gift.
> Will they accept him if he comes in a crowd?
> It is different for us.
> Wulf is on an island, I am on another.
> 5  The island is secure, surrounded by fens.
> There are savage men there on the isle:

Will they accept him if he comes in a crowd?
It is differently with us.
I suffered hopes of my Wulf's far travelling.
10  When it was rainy weather, and I sat weeping,
then the brave man clasped me in his arms,
that was both a joy to me, and hateful also.
Wulf, my Wulf, my hoping for you,
your few visits, a sorrowful mind
15  made me sick, not longing for food.
Do you hear, Eadwacer? Our wretched whelp
Wulf will carry away to the woods.
It is easy to wrench apart what was never joined –
our song together.

From the Old English, *Wulf and Eadwacer*, in the Exeter Book.
It is difficult to translate this poem for many reasons. There are
repeated lines (2 and 7, for example), but these are among the
most ambiguous of all. It is not at all clear who the 'he' is, or
'the brave man'. But even in its vagueness, the poem commu-
nicates a sense of tension powerfully.

**Text 24:** A riddle, not for the squeamish.

A young man came along where he knew her to be
standing in the corner of the hall. He went right up to her,
a lusty bachelor, lifted up his clothes
with his hands, thrust something stiff
under her girdle as she stood,
and had his way. Both of them shuddered.
The warrior was in a hurry, his goodly servant
was useful at times. Yet he, the strong one,
tired every time sooner than she did,

wearied of the business. Under her girdle
began to grow what often good men
love in their hearts and pay good money for.

From the Old English, *Riddle 54*, in the Exeter Book. Of
course, the solution is butter from the churn, to which the
young man has fitted the handle and spent an energetic few
minutes turning. If anything, the translation has toned down
the suggestiveness of the original, and this is one of the more
delicate of the suggestive riddles.

**Text 25:** The Battle of Chester.
Following the second conference between Augustine and the
British bishops, there is an impasse. The British bishops refuse
to give way on Easter, the Roman way of baptism, or to join in
evangelizing the English.

Augustine the man of God warned them threateningly
that if they did not wish to accept peace with their
brothers, they would be forced to accept war from their
enemies. And if they did not wish to preach the way of
life to the nation of the English, at their hands they
would in the end suffer the vengeance of death. In
every respect as he had prophesied, this was how it
happened by the agency of divine judgement.

The powerful king of the English, Æthelfrith ...
later on gathered a huge army against Chester ... and
conducted a great slaughter of that perfidious nation.
When he was about to start the battle, he saw the
priests who had gathered to pray to God for the soldiers
in the fight, standing in a safer place, and he asked who
they were and why they had gathered there. Most of

them were from the monastery of Bangor ... and they had a guard called Brocmail who was supposed to protect them from the swords of the barbarians while they were concentrating on their prayers. When Æthelfrith heard the reason for their coming he said, 'If they cry to their God against us, then they are fighting us even if they do not carry arms, opposing us with their prayers.' So he commanded them to be attacked first, and then destroyed the rest of the wicked army, though not without heavy losses to his own army. Of those who had come to pray, it is said that around twelve hundred men were killed in the battle, and only fifty got away ... So the prophecy of holy Augustine was fulfilled, even though he had been taken up into the heavenly kingdom long before, that those heretics should suffer the vengeance of temporal death because they had despised the offer of eternal salvation.

From Bede's Latin, *Ecclesiastical History*, book 2, chapter 2.

**Text 26:** St Cuthbert and the otters.

Cuthbert was sent for by the nun, widow, and mother of them all in Christ, Aebbe. He came, as invited, to the monastery which is called Coldingham, and staying there some days, did not relax his customary way of life but began to walk about by night on the seashore, keeping up his custom of singing as he kept vigil ... That man of God, with resolute mind, approaching the sea went into the waves up to his loin-cloth; and once he was soaked as far as his armpits by the tumultuous and billowing sea. When he came up out of the sea, he

prayed, bending his knees on the sandy part of the
shore, and immediately two little sea animals followed
in his footsteps, humbly prostrating themselves on the
earth, licking his feet, rolling upon them, wiping them
with their skins and warming them with their breath.
After completing this service and ministry, they
received his blessing and departed to their familiar
place in the waves of the sea. But the man of God
returned home at cockcrow, to join in communal
prayer with the brothers in the church of God.

From the Latin of the Anonymous *Life of St Cuthbert*, book 2,
chapter 3. The account of this miracle is much livelier in the
Anonymous *Life* than it is in Bede's version. Bede was not at
home with animals, apparently.

**Text 27:** St Cuthbert's last words.

He said, 'Always maintain peace and divine love
between yourselves ... And also keep concord with
other servants of Christ ... by no means deeming yourselves better than others in the same faith and life. But
with those who err from the unity of catholic peace,
whether in not celebrating Easter at the right time, or
in lives of perversity, let there be no communion. And
be aware and keep it in memory that if you have to
choose between two evils, I would much rather that
you took my bones from the tomb, and carried them
with you away from this place, and lived wherever God
might provide, than that you should agree to iniquity
and put your necks to the yoke of schismatics.

From Bede's Latin, *Life of St Cuthbert*, chapter 39. Nearly everything here is added to the Anonymous *Life*, and it is hard to imagine Cuthbert equating perverse living with the Celtic celebration of Easter. Curiously enough, the Lindisfarne community did take Cuthbert's bones from the tomb and carried them with them on their travels, when they were driven from the monastery by viking attacks over a century after this passage was written.

**Text 28:** St Aidan, according to Bede.

I have written thus of the character and deeds of Aidan, not at all praising or approving his inadequate knowledge of the proper observance of Easter. In fact, I greatly detest it as I have clearly proved in my book *De Temporibus* [On Times]. But as a truthful historian I have given an unadorned account of those things done by him or through him, commending those of his deeds worthy of praise and preserving their memory for the benefit of my readers. He had zeal for peace and love, self-restraint and humility. He overcame anger and greed, he despised pride and vainglory. He devoted himself to keeping as well as teaching the heavenly commandments, he was expert in reading and vigils. He used his authority as a priest to stand against the proud and powerful, and his kindness to comfort the sick and defend and relieve the poor. To put it briefly, so far as can be ascertained from those who knew him, he took care to overlook nothing of all that is written in the commands of the evangelists, apostles and prophets, but tried with all his power to carry them out. These things I greatly love and admire about the aforementioned Bishop Aidan, and that they are pleasing to God I have no doubt at all. But his failure to keep Easter at the proper time, either through ignorance of the canonical time or through being compelled by loyalty to the authority of his own people's custom – this I cannot approve or praise.

From Bede's Latin, *Ecclesiastical History*, book 3, chapter 17. At first sight, this passage and others make Bede appear to be a self-righteous prig. But he was genuinely trying to come to terms with a matter that caused him difficulties. He does not wish to deny the evidence, but it is evidence that undermines his world view. Honesty wins out.

## Text 29: The Council of Whitby.

The Easter controversy comes to a head after the death of Aidan, and after King Oswiu and his wife Eanflæd have celebrated Easter on different Sundays. Moreover, Alchfrith, Oswiu's son, had given land to monks of the Celtic persuasion to establish a monastery at Ripon. Then he apparently took it back and gave it to Wilfrid, the Roman advocate.

The question of Easter, the tonsure and other ecclesiastical matters came up again, and it was therefore decided to hold a council at Whitby, monastery of the woman devoted to God, Abbess Hild, to settle the matter. The two kings, Oswiu and Alchfrith, father and son, came; and Bishop Colman and his Irish clergy; Agilberht came with Agatho and Wilfrid, the priests. James and Romanus were on the Roman side, Abbess Hild and her people on the Irish side. Among the latter was the venerable Bishop Cedd who had been ordained by the Irish long before, and who acted as a most careful interpreter for both sides at the council.

First King Oswiu made the opening observation, that it was appropriate that those who served one God should keep one rule of life. Those who all hoped to be in one heavenly kingdom should not differ in the celebration of the heavenly sacraments. The thing now was to discover which was the truer tradition, and which therefore should be followed by all together.

He ordered his bishop Colman to speak first, as to the rite and its origin, as followed by the Irish. Colman said, 'The Easter which I observe I received from superiors, who sent me here as bishop. This is the Easter which all the Fathers of our church, men loved by God, are known to have celebrated ...'

Then Wilfrid, ordered by the king to speak, began, 'The Easter we keep is the one we see celebrated by all in Rome, where the blessed apostles Peter and Paul lived, taught, suffered and were buried; the one we observed in use by all in Italy, the one in Gaul, where we travelled for the purpose of learning and prayer; the same one is found in Africa, Asia, Egypt, and Greece, wherever the church of Christ has spread – we have learned that Easter is celebrated at one and the same time among different peoples and languages. The only people who stupidly fight against the whole world are these men and their colleagues in obstinacy, the Picts and the Britons, people of the two remotest islands in the ocean, and not even all of them!'

The fuller arguments are discussed. Then Wilfrid concludes.

'Even if your Columba was holy and powerful in working miracles – your Columba, and ours if he was in Christ – should he be preferred to the most blessed and chief of apostles, Peter, to whom the Lord said, "You are Peter, and on this rock I will build my church, and the gates of Hell will not overcome it, and I will give you the keys of the kingdom of heaven"?'

When Wilfrid had finished, King Oswiu said, 'Colman, is it true that the Lord said these words to Peter?' 'It is true, O king,' he said. The king went on and said, 'Do you have anything to indicate that a similar power was given to your Columba?' Colman replied, 'Nothing.' The king continued, 'Do you both agree in this, without dispute, that these words were spoken especially to Peter, and that the keys of the kingdom of heaven were given to him by the Lord?' They both agreed. Then the king concluded, 'Then I say to you, that if he is the keeper of the gates, I will not contradict him. Rather, I will try to obey him in everything, to the best of my knowledge and ability. Otherwise, when I come to the gates of the kingdom of heaven there may be nobody to open them, because the one who has been shown to hold the keys has turned away.'

When the king had said this, those sitting or standing there, high and low alike, indicated their agreement, and gave up their inadequate institutions and quickly replaced them with ones they recognized to be better.

From Bede's Latin, *Ecclesiastical History*, book 3, chapter 25. Bede does not disguise the arrogance in Wilfrid's voice. His contempt for St Columba is something the king apparently picks up. The slur on Columba's name is entirely unjustified, though as the sources show, Columba himself was not averse to playing power-games of a similar kind. Once again, this passage illustrates Roman disdain for the 'barbarians'.

**Text 30:** Bede's record of his life.

> I was born on the land of this monastery [of St Peter and St Paul, Monkwearmouth and Jarrow], and when I was seven years old I was given into the care of the most reverend Abbot Benedict, and then of Ceolfrid, by my kinsfolk, to be educated. Since that time I have passed my entire life in this monastery, giving myself wholly to the study of the scripture. In the course of observance of the discipline of the monastic Rule, and the daily singing of the services in the church, it has always been a pleasure to me to learn or teach or write. I was made deacon at the age of nineteen, at thirty I was ordained priest, both times through the ministry of the most reverend Bishop John at the direction of Abbot Ceolfrid. From the time I was ordained priest until I was fifty-nine, I have taken care, for my own benefit and that of my brothers, to compile brief extracts from the works of the venerable Fathers on the holy scriptures, and to add notes for clarification on their sense and meaning.

From Bede's Latin, *Ecclesiastical History*, book 5, chapter 24. Bede goes on to list most of his books, nearly all of which are known from medieval copies. The list is considerable, and any one of the books shows a wealth of learning.

**Text 31:** Bede's self-justification.

I beg you by all means to show this, my letter of justification, to our highly-religious and most learned brother David, so that he may read it before our venerable lord and father, Bishop Wilfrid. Since he was present and listening when I was so insultingly attacked before, he should now also, by listening and judging, understand how I have patiently endured those same unmerited insults. And I ask that same David publicly that according to the example of a boy of the same name, he zealously try to put to flight the fury of the spirit ... by a well-chosen apology ... At that meal when he tried so hard to make me appear guilty of the cup [i.e. drunkenness], he, who should have made himself less blameworthy by intensive study, was unable to carry out his intent, since he never realized that it was my opinion which he praised. It is truly said, 'Surely the serpent will bite without enchantment, and the babbler is no better.'

From Bede's Latin, *Letter to Plegwine*, section 17, in the translation of C. W. Jones.

**Text 32:** The story of Cædmon, from Hild's monastery at Whitby.

In this abbess's monastery there was a certain brother singularly honoured and dignified by a divine gift, in that he habitually composed suitable songs which related to religion and piety. So that, whatever he learned from religious writings through scholars, the same he produced after a space of time in verse of

the greatest sweetness and inspirational quality in well-
turned English. And through his songs, the minds of
many were often kindled with contempt for the world
and desire to join the spiritual life. Many others after
him in England began to compose religious songs, but
none could do it quite like him, because it was 'not
from man nor by human means' that he learned the art
of poetry, but he was divinely helped and received the
art by the gift of God. Because of that, he never composed songs of fiction or idle pleasure, but only such as
related to piety was it appropriate for his pious tongue
to sing.

This man was established in secular life until he
had reached advanced age and he never learned any
songs. Because of this, whenever it was decided that
there should be a party and that they should all sing in
turn to the harp, he often got up in shame from the
feast and went home. On one particular occasion he
did this, that is, left the house where the party was, and
went out to the cattle shed where it was his responsibility to look after the animals for the night. Then
when he lay down to rest at the appropriate time and
slept, a certain man appeared to him in a dream, and
addressed and greeted him, and called him by his
name, 'Cædmon, sing me something.' He answered
and said, 'I don't know how to sing anything, and for
that very reason, I went out of tonight's party and came
here, because I do not know how to sing anything.'
The one who was speaking to Cædmon said again, 'But
you are able to sing to me.' So Cædmon said, 'What
must I sing?' He said, 'Sing me the creation.' When he
got this answer, he immediately started to sing in praise

of God, words and verses that he had never heard, and
this is their sequence:

Now we ought to praise the Guardian of the kingdom of
    heaven,
the might of the Creator and his understanding,
the works of the Father of glory, how he, of each wonder
the eternal Lord, established a beginning.
He first created for the sons of the earth
heaven as a roof, the holy Creator.
Then the world, the Guardian of humankind,
the eternal Lord, afterwards created
the land for the people, the almighty Lord.

Then he got up from his sleep and all the things he had
sung in his sleep he retained firmly in his memory,
and quickly to those words he added more words in the
same style, of songs dear to God. He went in the morning to the reeve who was his master and told him the
sort of gift he had received. He took him immediately
to the abbess, and told it to her. She commanded all the
most learned men and the teachers to assemble, and
commanded him to tell the dream and sing the song in
their presence. Then the judgement of all, as to what
the gift was and where it had come from, was sought.
They all said (which was actually the case) that a spiritual gift had been given to Cædmon by God himself.
Then they read out a holy story and told him some
words of spiritual instruction, asking him, if he was able,
to change these into delightful verse. When he had
received this material he went home to his house and
came back in the morning, and giving them back what

they had given him, sang the best decorated verse. The
abbess embraced and praised the gift of God in the
man, and she urged and instructed him that he should
leave his secular life, and become a monk, and he readily accepted that. She received him and his goods into
the monastery and inducted him into the community of
God's servants. She commanded him to be taught the
whole course of sacred history and scripture, and he,
retaining in his memory all the things that he could
learn from listening, like an animal chewing the cud,
transformed them into the sweetest verse. And his song
and verse were so delightful to hear, that his very teachers wrote down what he said and learned it. He sang
first of all about the creation of the world and the origin
of humankind and the history of Genesis (the first book
of Moses); next about the exodus of the Israelite people
out of the land of Egypt and afterwards the entry into
the Promised Land; and about many other accounts
in the canonical books of Holy Scripture. And about
Christ's incarnation and his suffering, and his ascension
into the heavens, and the coming of the Holy Spirit,
and the teaching of the apostles. And next he composed many songs about the future Day of Judgement
and about the fearfulness of the torments of hell and
the sweetness of the heavenly kingdom. And likewise
he composed many others about the divine judgements
and blessings. In all these he diligently took care to
draw people away from love of sin and evil deeds and to
incite in them love and desire for good deeds. For he
was a very pious man, humbly devoted to the discipline
of the monastic rule, and he became zealously incensed
with those who wished to act otherwise. For this reason

he closed and ended his life with a beautiful ending.

So when the time of his death and departure approached, for forty days before he was afflicted and burdened with bodily illness, yet not so much so that he could not walk or talk. Nearby was the infirmary, where it was the custom to put the sick and dying, and look after them all there. Then he asked his servant, at evening of the night on which he was to die, to prepare a place for him to rest there. The servant wondered why he asked him to do this because it did not seem to him that Cædmon's death was all that near. He nevertheless did as he was asked. And when he went to bed there, he joined in cheerful fashion with those who were talking and joking there. When it was midnight, he asked if they had the eucharist in the place. They answered and said, 'What need do you have for the eucharist? Your death cannot be so close as even now you are cheerfully and gladly talking with us.' He said again, 'Bring me the eucharist.' When he had it in his hands he asked whether they were all peacefully and happily disposed and without bitterness towards him. And they by reply asked if he was happily disposed towards them. Then he answered and said, 'My brothers, my dear brothers, I am very happily disposed towards you and all God's people.' And thus he was strengthened and provided with spiritual food for the entry into the next life. Still he asked how near the time was for the brothers to get up and give praise to God and sing the dawn office. They answered, 'Not long now.' He said, 'Good. We ought to wait for that time.' And then he asked them to sign him with Christ's cross, laid his head on his pillow, and slept for a short time. And thus it came about that as he had served the Lord with a pure and innocent spirit, so also he gave up the earth in a similarly serene death, and entered his Lord's presence. And the tongue which had composed so many saving words in praise of the Creator, said its last words in his praise; and he signed himself and ended by entrusting himself to God's hands. Thus it is seen that he knew the time of his own death from what we have heard said.

From the Old English translation of Bede's *Ecclesiastical History*, book 4, chapter 24. There are some passages here which have been smoothed out in the translation. But this is a story which is told well in the Old English. The crucial passage introducing and including Bede's version of the *Hymn* in Latin is given here:

Having received this response [to sing of the beginning of created things], he immediately began to sing in praise of God the creator verses that he had never heard, of which this is the gist:

Now we must praise the guardian of the kingdom of heaven, the power of the creator and his understanding, the works of the Father of glory: how he who is the eternal God became the author of all wonders; who first created the heavens as the rooftop for the sons of men, then afterwards, almighty guardian of humankind, created the earth.

This is the gist, not the order of the words, which he sang as he slept. It is not possible for songs, however well composed, to be translated literally from one language into another without loss to their beauty and dignity.

**Text 33:** Selections from *Beowulf*.
Grendel attacks the Danes.

> The powerful spirit, Grendel, miserably
> endured this time, he who lived in the darkness
> miserably endured the daily sound of joy,
> loud in the hall. There was the music of the harp,
> 90 the clear song of the poet. He who knew how to tell it
> told of the creation of people long ago,
> said that the Almighty made the earth,
> the beautiful country as far as the sea's limit,
> established the victorious sun and moon,
> 95 lamps to lighten dwellers on the land;
> and adorned the earth's surface
> with boughs and leaves; and also created life
> for all kinds of living creatures that move about.
> In this way the noble men lived happily
> 100 in joy, until a certain hellish enemy
> began to commit crime.
> The grim spirit was called Grendel,
> a famous wanderer in the outlands, who occupied
>     the wastelands
> the fen and its stronghold. The unhappy man
> 105 occupied the homeland of the monstrous race for the
>     time
> after the Creator had condemned them
> as Cain's close family – he, the eternal Lord
> avenged that death, when Cain killed Abel;

he got no joy from that feud, but the Lord
110 banished him far away from humankind for the crime.
From him all the evil brood of monsters and elves
were bred, and all evil spirits,
likewise all the giants, who contended against God
for a long time. God requited them.
115 After night fell Grendel left his place to find
the high house, to discover how the Ring-Danes
had left it after the beer-drinking.
He found in it a troop of princely retainers
sleeping after the banquet: they knew no sorrow,
120 no human misery. The evil creature,
grim and greedy, savage and cruel,
was soon ready, and from the resting-place seized
thirty warriors. He went from there
exulting in his catch, with an abundance of the dead,
125 back home to seek his own surroundings.
Then in the morning, the earliest part of the day,
Grendel's act of war became evident to the men.
After feasting, the sound of mourning arose,
a great morning-cry. The prince,
130 the doughty prince proved by time, the mighty
    and powerful one,
sat miserable, endured and suffered the loss of his
    retainers,
after they followed the hateful tracks
of the accursed spirit ...
    It was a long time;
the friendly lord of the Danes suffered torment
for twelve years, all the miseries
of great afflictions. It became widely known
150 among warriors, the sons of men,

in sad songs, that Grendel fought with Hrothgar
for that time, carried out hateful deeds of malice,
crimes and feuding for many seasons,
a constant battle ...
170 That was a great misery, grief of heart
to the friendly lord of the Danes. Many powerful men
often sat round in counsel; they considered what
    would be
the best course for the brave men to take
against the awful horrors.
175 Sometimes they promised sacrifices,
offered vows in words at heathen shrines,
so that they might get help from the slayer of souls
for the distress of the people. Such was their custom,
the hope of the heathen. They remembered
180 hell in their hearts; they did not know the Lord,
the Judge of deeds; they were not aware of the Lord
    God,
nor indeed were they able to praise the Lord of the
    heavens,
the Lord of glory. Woe it is for those
who through persistent enmity thrust their souls
185 into the embrace of the fire, never to expect
    consolation,
never any change! Well it is for those who are allowed
to seek the Lord after the day of death,
and seek for protection in the embrace of the Father.

In the song of creation mentioned here, and indeed in the story of Cain and Abel, there are many echoes of the Bible. 'All kinds of living creatures that move about' is a distinct echo of Genesis 1:25. That sets the scene for the Romans passage to be recalled: that people knew God from what was created, but turned away from him to idols. Here we see the desperation of the Danes, faced with Grendel's attacks. The poet shows all possible sympathy for them, but has to warn that the logical conclusion was that they were putting themselves in greater danger of eternal damnation. The Anglo-Saxons frequently fell into apostasy in times of war, famine and plague, and the warning here would not have been missed.

Hrothgar warns Beowulf.

It is a marvel to tell

1725   how mighty God in his infinite wisdom
      shares out wisdom and abilities, homes and noble
        gifts,
      to humanity: he possesses control over everything.
      Sometimes he has everything turn out
      according to the desire and conception of a man
        of famous family;

1730   he grants him to have, and keep, earthly joy,
      in his homeland a stronghold of men,
      makes subject to him parts of the world,
      a vast kingdom, to such a degree that he cannot,
      for his folly, imagine an end to it all.

1735   He lives in abundance, old age and illness
      hinder him not at all, and neither evil sorrow
      darkens his mind, nor does enmity,
      sword-hatred, show itself anywhere; but all the
        world goes
      just how he wishes. He knows nothing of the darker
        side,

1740   until in his heart a seed of pride
      grows and flourishes; then the guardian of the soul,

the protector, sleeps, and the sleep is too deep,
bound by busyness, and the killer is very close,
the killer who shoots wickedly from a bow.
1745 Then the man is hit in the heart with a bitter arrow,
pierced under his protection, and he cannot protect
    himself
from the accursed spirit's perverse and strange
    promptings.
It seems to him that what he has had all this time is
    not enough,
he starts to become grasping and savagely covetous,
he does not give out as he promised
1750 the studded rings, and he overlooks
and neglects his destiny which God, the Lord
    of glory,
gave him before, his share of honour.
In the end it inevitably happens
that the failing body declines and decays,
1755 the doomed man dies, and another inherits,
someone who gladly gives out treasures,
the ancient valuables of noblemen, and fears
    no terrors.
Guard yourself against miserliness, my dear Beowulf,
best of men, and choose for yourself the better part,
1760 eternal counsels. Do not focus on pride,
glorious warrior! Now for a while
your strength is famous; it will soon happen
that age or sword come between you and your power,
or the snatch of fire, or the surge of waves,
1765 or the grip of the sword, or the flight of the arrow,
or terrible age. Or the brightness of your eyes
will fail and grow dim. It will suddenly happen,
noble man, that you are overcome by death.

There are all kinds of biblical echoes here, not only from Ephesians, but also from Ecclesiastes, for example. In Ecclesiastes, it is regarded as the height of folly that a person should grasp and toil only to die and leave all his wealth to someone else. There are quite a good number of Old English sermons which itemize the various ways you can die: this rather macabre fascination with death develops into an obsession in later medieval literature.

Beowulf's funeral.

Then the people of the Geats constructed
a burial mound on the hillside. It was high and wide,
visible to seafarers from a long way off.
And they built in ten days a monument
3160 to the man bold in battle, they surrounded
the remains from the fire with a wall, with all the
skill
that the wisest of men could devise.
They put inside it rings and gems,
all the adornments that hostile men
3165 had formerly taken from the [dragon's] hoard.
They abandoned the treasures of noblemen for the
earth to keep,
gold in the dirt – where it still lives
as useless to men as it was before.
Then men brave in battle, the sons of princes,
3170 twelve in all, rode around the mound.
Their desire was to make known their sorrow, and
to lament the king,
to compose a memorial poem and to speak of the
man.
They praised his nobility and his deeds of courage,

honoured his excellences. It is right that a man
should so

3175 praise his friendly lord in words,
and love him in his heart, when he must be
led forth from the home of the body.
In this proper way the people of the Geats, retainers,
mourned their lord's death;

3180 they said that he had been among worldly kings
the mildest of men, and the most merciful,
the most gentle with his people, and the most
desirous of praise.

There are many interesting features here. While the poet
faithfully records heathen burial customs, he nevertheless feels
obliged to comment that gold buried in the earth is useless.
And he reinforces that view (if as I think the hoard from
which the treasure is taken is the dragon's) by showing that the
warriors just took treasure from one hoard and put it straight
into another. What a waste of time. Beowulf's epitaph from
the warriors is also odd. To have spoken of Attila or
Theodoric, or Æthelfrith of Bernicia, or any of the great historical heathen kings as mild, merciful and gentle, would have
had them turning in their graves. Eager for praise, yes, but not
gentle! This again shows how the poet wishes to judge the
hero by Christian standards. Moses, it will be recalled, was
'the humblest of men', Numbers 12:3. The poet wanted his
Christian audience to see how heathens could behave in ways
which would be appropriate for Christians, and thus be 'a law
to themselves'.

All from the Old English poem, *Beowulf*.

**Text 34:** *The Dream of the Rood.*

Listen. I want to describe the best of dreams
that came to me in the middle of the night
when humans capable of speech kept their beds.
It seemed to me that I saw a superb tree,
5   brightest of trees, caught up in the clouds,
surrounded with light. All that sign was
drenched with gold, gems gleamed
gracious at the surface of the earth, and similarly there
were five
up on the cross-beam. Armies of angels beautiful from
first creation,
10   gazed there; that was surely not the gallows of a felon,
but the spirits of the holy ones, people on earth,
and all this marvellous creation gazed upon it there.
Wondrous was the tree of victory, and I was stained
with sins,
injured by iniquities. I saw the tree of glory
15   graced with garments, joyously shining,
adorned with gold. Jewels nobly
covered the tree of the Lord.
Yet through the gold, I was able to perceive
the ancient strife of enemies, when it began for the
first time
20   to bleed on the right hand side. I was devastated with
sorrows,
afraid because of the beautiful vision. I saw the
shimmering sign
change colour and garments: sometimes it was
dripping with wetness,
drenched with the flow of blood; sometimes it was
adorned with treasure.

So lying there for a long time, I gazed, sorrowing,
25    upon the Saviour's tree,
until I heard that it spoke.
The best of trees began to speak these words:
'That was a long time ago – I can still remember it –
when I was cut down at the edge of the wood,
30    removed from my stem. There strong enemies seized
        me,
made me a spectacle for themselves, ordered me to
    raise up their criminals;
warriors carried me there on their shoulders until they
    set me up on a hill,
many enemies fixed me there. Then I saw the Lord of
    mankind
hasten, with great zeal, when he wished to climb upon
    me.
35    I did not dare bend or break there,
go against the Lord's word, even when I saw
the surface of the earth shake. I could have killed
all the enemies, yet I stood firm.
Then the young hero who was God almighty stripped
    himself,
40    strong and resolute; he climbed up on the high
        gallows,
brave in the sight of many, when he wished to redeem
    humanity.
I trembled when the warrior embraced me, yet I did
    not dare bow to the earth,
fall flat on the ground, but I had to stand firm.
I was raised as a cross. I hung up the powerful king,
45    the Lord of the heavens, I did not dare bow down.
They pierced me with bloody nails, and the wounds
    are yet visible on me,

the gaping marks of malicious strokes: I did not dare
   harm any of them.
They abused us both together. I was absolutely
   drenched with blood
which spouted from the warrior's side after he sent on
   his spirit.

50  I have experienced many dreadful things
   on that hill. I saw the Lord of hosts
   savagely stretched out. Darkness covered
   the bright radiance of the Lord's body,
   covered it with clouds; shadow went forth,

55  dark under the clouds. All creation wept,
   lamented the King's death. Christ was on the cross.
   Then from afar men hurried
   to the Prince. I gazed on it all.
   I was overcome with sorrows, yet I bowed humbly to
      hands of those men

60  with much courage. There they took almighty God
      down,
   relieved him of that heavy torment. The warriors
      abandoned me
   to stand drenched with moisture. I was wounded to
      death with arrows.
   There they laid down the one weary of limb, they
      stood at head and feet,
   and gazed on the Lord of heaven; and he rested there
      for a time,

65  weary after the great conflict. Then, in the sight of the
      killers,
   the warriors made him a grave, carved it out of bright
      stone,
   and put in it the Lord of victories. Then they sang a
      dirge,

miserable in the evening, when they, weary, wanted to go away

from the glorious Lord. He remained there with no company.

70　So, weeping, we stood there for a long time
fixed in place. The voice of warriors
faded away; the body went cold,
the gracious house of the spirit. Then we were cut down,
all of us were felled to the ground – that was a fearful thing!

75　We were buried in a deep pit. Yet the Lord's retainers
and friends heard of us.
They adorned me with gold and silver.
Now you have been able to hear, my beloved hero,
that I have experienced severe sorrows

80　from the deeds of the inhabitants of iniquity. Now the time has come
when people on earth and all this marvellous creation,
far and wide, honour me,
and pray to this sign. On me the Son of God
suffered for a time. Therefore, glorious now,

85　I tower under the heavens, and I am able to heal
each one in whom is fear towards me.
Formerly I was made into the severest of tortures,
most hateful to the people, before I opened to them,
to bearers of speech, the right way of life.

90　Listen – the Lord of glory, the guardian of the kingdom of heaven,
then honoured me over the trees of the forest,
just as he honoured Mary herself,
his mother, before all people,

God almighty honoured her above all the race of
   women.
95 Now I command you, my beloved hero,
   that you tell this vision to people,
   reveal in words that it is the tree of glory
   on which almighty God suffered
   for the many sins of humankind
100 and for Adam's deeds of old.
   He tasted death there, yet the Lord rose again
   by his mighty power to aid all people.
   He then ascended to the heavens. He, the Lord
      himself,
   God almighty, and his angels with him,
105 will come back here to this earth
   to seek mankind on the day of judgement,
   when he, the one who has the right to judge,
   wishes to judge each one according
   to what they have earned in this passing life.
110 No one will be able to be without fear there,
   because of the word that the Lord will say:
   he will ask before the multitude where the man might
      be
   who for the sake of the Lord's name would be willing
   to taste bitter death, as he formerly did on the cross.
115 They will then be afraid, and few will have thought
   what they will be able to say to Christ.
   No one who carries within their breast the best of
      signs
   need be over-fearful there,
   for by means of the cross each soul
120 who intends to dwell with the Lord
   must seek the kingdom in the paths of the earth.

Happy in mind, I prayed then to the cross
with great zeal, there where I was alone,
without company. My mind was excited,
125 eager to be off on the journey, having experienced
many a time of longing. Now my hope in life
is that I alone might have recourse to the tree of victory
more often than all others,
and honour it well. The desire for that
130 is great in my mind, and my hope of protection is
directed towards the cross. I do not have many –
or any –
powerful friends on earth, for they have all
passed away from worldly joys, and gone to be with the
King of glory;
they live now with the Father on high,
135 dwell in glory, and I look forward
each day to the time when the Lord's cross,
that I saw previously here on earth,
will fetch me from this passing life
and bring me to where there is great bliss,
140 joys in heaven, where the Lord's people
are seated at the banquet, where there is eternal bliss –
and then set me down where I for ever after may be
allowed
to remain in glory, richly to enjoy with the holy ones
heavenly pleasures. May the Lord be my friend
145 who here on earth formerly suffered
on the gallows tree for the sins of men.
He redeemed us, gave us life
and a heavenly home. Hope was renewed
gloriously and blissfully, for those who endured
burning there:

150 the Son was victorious on that expedition,
     powerful and successful, when he came with a host,
     a whole troop of spirits, into God's kingdom,
     the almighty sole ruler, to the bliss of angels
     and all the holy ones who formerly had dwelt in heaven
155 and remained in glory, when their Lord, almighty God,
     came back to where his home was.

From the Old English poem, *The Dream of the Rood*.

**Text 35:** Verse from the cross at Ruthwell.

> God almighty stripped himself
> when he wished to climb upon the gallows,
> brave before all people.
> I did not dare bow.
>
> I raised up the powerful king,
> the Lord of heaven, I did not dare fall down.
> They abused us both together. I was drenched with
>   blood
> that spouted from ...
>
> Christ was on the cross.
> Yet from afar men came hurrying
> noble ones to the One. I gazed on it all.
> I was overcome with sorrows, yet I bowed ...
>
> ... was wounded with arrows.
> They laid down the one weary of limb, they stood at
>   head and feet,
> gazed on there ...

From the Old English runic inscription on the Ruthwell Cross. The text is badly damaged, as over the centuries the cross has been smashed, used as paving slabs, resurrected and pieced together wrongly. Despite all this, the similarity of the inscription with lines 39–64 of *The Dream of the Rood* is unmistakable. As the text runs up and down two sides of the cross, preachers at the site could probably tell who were the inattentive listeners because of their sore necks.

# SOURCES AND FURTHER READING

# CHAPTER 1

The best history of Anglo-Saxon England is by F. M. Stenton, *Anglo-Saxon England*, 3rd ed. (Oxford: The Oxford History of England, Volume 2, Clarendon Press, 1971). Also excellent is Peter Hunter Blair, *An Introduction to Anglo-Saxon England*, 2nd ed. (Cambridge: Cambridge University Press, 1977). The standard edition of Bede's *Historia Ecclesiastica Gentis Anglorum*, in Latin with facing-page English translation, is B. Colgrave and R. A. B. Mynors, *Bede's Ecclesiastical History of the English People* (Oxford: Oxford Medieval Texts, Clarendon Press, 1969). There is also a good translation in Penguin, *A History of the English Church and People*, trans. Leo Sherley-Price, revised by R. E. Latham (Harmondsworth: Penguin, 1968). Bede's *Life* and the Anonymous *Life* of St Cuthbert are both edited and translated by Bertram Colgrave, *Two Lives of Saint Cuthbert* (Cambridge: Cambridge University Press, 1940). For a useful collection of Anglo-Saxon literature translated from Latin and Old English, see D. Whitelock, ed., *English Historical Documents Vol. I, c. 500–1042* (London: Eyre and Spottiswoode, 1955).

## CHAPTER 2

Place-names are explored by Kenneth Cameron, *English Place Names*, 3rd ed. (London: Batsford, 1996), and in the ever-growing number of volumes produced by the English Place-Name Society. Scandinavian heathenism is explored by John McKinnell, *Both One and Many: Essays on Change and Variety in Late Norse Heathenism* (Rome: Il Calamo, 1994).

Bede's work on times and dates is edited, with a good introduction but no translation, by C. W. Jones, *Bedae Opera de Temporibus* (Cambridge MA: The Mediaeval Academy of America, 1943). An excellent collection of essays on St Cuthbert, including one on the runes on his coffin by R. I. Page, is Gerald Bonner, David Rollason and Clare Stancliffe, eds., *St Cuthbert, his Cult and his Community to A.D. 1200* (Woodbridge: The Boydell Press, 1989).

The *Solomon and Saturn* poems are edited by Robert J. Menner, *The Poetical Dialogues of Solomon and Saturn* (New York and London: Modern Language Association of America: Monograph Series, 13, Oxford University Press, 1941), and by E. V. K. Dobbie, *The Anglo-Saxon Minor Poems* (New York: The Anglo-Saxon Poetic Records VI, Columbia University Press, 1942). The *Metrical Charms* are also edited by Dobbie in *The Anglo-Saxon Minor Poems*. There are two sets of proverbial poems in Old English entitled *Maxims*, one in *The Exeter Book*, edited by G. P. Krapp and E. V. K. Dobbie, (New York: The Anglo-Saxon Poetic Records III, Columbia University Press, 1934) and the other in a manuscript of the Cottonian collection in *The Anglo-Saxon Minor Poems*. The *Medicina de Quadrupedibus* is edited by H. J. De Vriend (London: The Early English Text Society, 1984). The Sutton Hoo ship burial was discovered in 1939 near Woodbridge in Suffolk. The likely date of the ceremony (there is apparently no body) is around 625. The grave goods include weapons, coins from France, bowls of Byzantine, Coptic and Celtic types, two spoons with Greek lettering, and some other items difficult to identify, but clearly symbolic of status. The excavation and analysis is published in four parts in three large volumes, R. L. S. Bruce-Mitford, *The Sutton Hoo Ship Burial* (London: British Museum Press, 1975–83).

# CHAPTER 3

Tacitus's *Germania* is available in Penguin, translated by H. Mattingly, revised by S. A. Handford (Harmondsworth: Penguin, 1979). *The Anglo-Saxon Chronicle* gives the date of the Anglo-Saxon invasion as AD 449. The *Chronicle* is edited and translated by G. N. Garmonsway (London: Everyman's Library, Dent, 1954). The Old English poem *The Ruin* in the Exeter Book refers to the remains of Roman Bath as *enta geweorc*, 'the work of giants'. Nottingham is *Snotengeham* in Domesday Book (1086). The *De Excidio Britanniae* of Gildas was written around 540, and is edited and translated by Michael Winterbottom, *Gildas: The Ruin of Britain and Other Documents* (London: Arthurian Period Sources, vol. 7, Phillimore, 1978). For Nennius' *Historia Brittonum*, see John Morris's edition and translation, *Nennius: British History and The Welsh Annals* in the Arthurian Period Sources (vol. 8, 1980). J. A. Giles edited a rather various collection of historical works as *Six Old English Chronicles* (London: George Bell, 1885); the translation of Gildas' contorted Latin is taken from this edition. The Old English poem *Andreas* is the apocryphal story of the apostle and saint, Andrew, one of Jesus' original twelve disciples. St Andrew goes to preach the gospel to, and rescue St Matthew from, cannibals in Mermedonia. There is an early Greek manuscript of the story and two Latin versions. The Old English poem seems to have been translated from a third Latin version, and has many adaptations to suit the Anglo-Saxon audience. *Andreas* is edited by K. R. Brooks (Oxford: Clarendon Press, 1961) and translated in S. A. J. Bradley, *Anglo-Saxon Poetry* (London: Everyman's Library, Dent, 1982). The *Life* of Wilfrid is edited and translated by Bertram Colgrave, *The Life of Bishop Wilfrid by Eddius Stephanus* (Cambridge: Cambridge University Press, 1927). The Old English poem, *The Battle of Maldon*, relating to the battle on the Essex coast between the English and the vikings in AD 991, is edited by Donald Scragg (Manchester: Manchester University Press, 1981). Byrhtnoth is the commander of the English forces, and he lets the vikings cross the causeway from the island of Northey to the mainland for a pitched battle. Byrhtnoth is killed, and some English warriors take to their heels. Ælfric's *Lives of the Saints*, a series of homilies on the saints for their festival days, is edited and translated in two volumes by W. W. Skeat (London: Early English Text Society, 1881–1900). Bede's *Letter to Ecgberht* was written in 734, not long before Bede died, and is edited by Charles Plummer, *Venerabilis Baedae Opera Historica*, vol. I (Oxford: Clarendon Press, 1896, pp. 405–423). The Paris Psalter contains a prose version of Psalms 1–50 and a verse translation of Psalms 51–150. The verse is edited by G. P. Krapp (New York: The Anglo-Saxon Poetic Records vol. V, Columbia University Press, 1932). Ælfric's *Preface to Genesis*, where he outlines his hesitations about translating the Old Testament, is edited in Bruce Mitchell and Fred C. Robinson, *A Guide to Old English*, 5th ed. (Oxford: Blackwell, 1992).

# CHAPTER 4

Ælfric's *Colloquy* is edited in Bruce Mitchell and Fred C. Robinson, *A Guide to Old English* (see chapter 3 above). The *Benedictine Rule* has been translated many times, but a good translation is Justin McCann, *The Rule of Saint Benedict* (London: Sheed and Ward, 1976). For some details on Whitby Abbey and the earlier foundation under Abbess Hild, see Christine E. Fell, 'Hild, abbess of Streonæshalch' in *Hagiography and Medieval Literature: A Symposium*, ed. H. Bekker-Nielsen (Odense: Odense University Press, 1981), pp. 76–89. On the role of the monasteries in the conversion of Anglo-Saxon England, see J. Campbell, 'The First Century of Christianity in England', in *Essays in Anglo-Saxon History* (London: Hambledon Press, 1986), and more recently R. Fletcher, *The Conversion of Europe: From Paganism to Christianity 371–1386 AD* (London: HarperCollins, 1997). For the archaeology of monasteries and churches, see essays in D. M. Wilson, ed., *The Archaeology of Anglo-Saxon England* (Cambridge: Cambridge University Press, 1981). On manuscripts, see Michelle P. Brown, *Anglo-Saxon Manuscripts* (London: The British Library, 1991). An accessible book on Alcuin is E. S. Duckett, *Alcuin, Friend of Charlemagne* (New York: Macmillan, 1951); for a translation of some of his letters, see S. Allott, *Alcuin of York: His Life and Letters* (York: Sessions, 1974). The standard text of Alcuin's letters is by E. Dümmler in *Monumenta Germaniae Historica, Epistolae*, vol. IV. Alcuin's use of number symbolism is briefly discussed by W. F. Bolton, *Alcuin and Beowulf: An Eighth-Century View* (London: Arnold, 1979). The Exeter Book is edited by Krapp and Dobbie in the Anglo-Saxon Poetic Records series, vol. III, but also by Bernard J. Muir, *The Exeter Anthology of Old English*

*Poetry: An Edition of Exeter Dean and Chapter MS 3501*, 2 vols (Exeter: University of Exeter Press, 1994). For a general treatment of the role, status and activities of women in the Anglo-Saxon period, the best book is *Women in Anglo-Saxon England and the Impact of 1066*, by Christine Fell with Cecily Clark and Elizabeth Williams (London: British Museum Publications, 1984). An excellent collection of essays on the subject of women in general and the elegies in particular, is *New Readings on Women in Old English Literature*, edited by Helen Damico and Alexandra Hennessey Olsen (Bloomington: Indiana University Press, 1990). The essay by Fell in *The Cambridge Companion to Old English Literature* edited by Malcolm Godden and Michael Lapidge (Cambridge: Cambridge University Press, 1991) is also important. And Henk Aertsen's on *Wulf and Eadwacer* in *Companion to Old English Poetry*, edited by Henk Aertsen and Rolf H. Bremmer (Amsterdam: VU University Press, 1994) is valuable. These two collections of essays contain many useful studies of Old English literature. A complete edition of the so-called elegies is Anne L. Klinck, *The Old English Elegies: A Critical Edition and Genre Study* (Montreal: McGill-Queen's University Press, 1992). The Old English Riddles are translated, with a useful introduction, by C. Williamson, *A Feast of Creatures: Anglo-Saxon Riddle Songs* (London: Scolar, 1982), though he rather irritatingly does not use the numbering of riddles established by Krapp and Dobbie in their *Exeter Book* edition. A wide-ranging treatment of the genre is M. Bryant, *Riddles Ancient and Modern* (London: Hutchinson, 1983).

# CHAPTER 5

There are many books on Bede. Probably the best general works are P. Hunter Blair's *The World of Bede* (London: Secker and Warburg, 1970, recently reprinted by Cambridge University Press in paperback) and *Northumbria in the Days of Bede* (London, 1976). There is a good short introduction to Bede's significance as a Christian thinker in B. Ward, *The Venerable Bede* (London: Geoffrey Chapman, 1990). Two collections of critical essays are A. Hamilton Thompson, ed., *Bede, His Life, Times and Writings* (Oxford: Oxford University Press, 1935) and G. Bonner, ed., *Famulus Christi: Essays in Commemoration of the Thirteenth Centenary of the Birth of the Venerable Bede* (London: SPCK, 1976). The Lindisfarne Gospels are discussed and illustrated by Janet Backhouse, *The Lindisfarne Gospels* (Oxford: Phaidon, 1981). The *Letter to Plegwine* is edited by C. W. Jones in *Bedae Opera de Temporibus* (see chapter 2 above). The *Life* of Wilfrid is edited by Colgrave (see chapter 3 above).

# CHAPTER 6

There are many technical studies of Cædmon's *Hymn*. The text is edited by A. H. Smith, *Three Northumbrian Poems*, rev. ed. (Exeter: Methuen's Old English Library, 1978). A good study is C. L. Wrenn, 'The Poetry of Cædmon', *Proceedings of the British Academy*, 32 (1946), pp. 277–95. Others include: E. G. Stanley, 'The Oldest English Poetry Now Extant', *Poetica* (Tokyo), 2 (1974), pp. 1–24; U. Schwab, 'The Miracles of Caedmon – Revisited', *Atti dell' Accademia Peloritana*, Classe di lettere, filosofia e belle arti, 59 (1985), pp. 5–36; A. Orchard, 'Poetic Inspiration and Prosaic Translation: The Making of

Cædmon's Hymn', in *Studies in English Language and Literature:
'Doubt Wisely', Papers in Honour of E. G. Stanley*, edited by
M. J. Toswell and E. M. Tyler (London: Routledge, 1996), pp.
402–22; G. R. Isaac, 'The Date and Origin of Cædmon's
Hymn', *Neuphilologische Mitteilungen*, 98 (1997), pp. 217–28;
and D. R. Howlett, 'The Theology of Cædmon's Hymn', *Leeds
Studies in English*, New Series 7 (1974), pp. 1–12. The scholar
quoted is K. S. Kiernan, 'Reading Cædmon's "Hymn" with
Someone Else's Glosses', *Representations*, 32 (1990), pp.
157–74. The manuscripts are discussed by E. V. K. Dobbie, *The
Manuscripts of Cædmon's Hymn and Bede's Death Song: With a
Critical Text of the Epistola Cuthberti de obitu Bedæ*, (New York:
Columbia University Studies in English and Comparative
Literature, 128, 1937).

# CHAPTER 7

*St Erkenwald* is edited by Sir I. Gollancz (Oxford: Early English
Text Society, 1922) and translated by B. Stone, *The Owl
and the Nightingale, Cleanness, St Erkenwald* (Harmondsworth:
Penguin, 1971). There is only one truly satisfactory edition of
*Beowulf*, that of F. Klaeber, *Beowulf and the Fight at Finnsburg*,
3rd ed. (Boston, MA: Heath, 1950). The information relating
to Panzer's work is from Klaeber, pp. xiii–xiv. C. L. Wrenn's
edition, revised by W. F. Bolton (London: Harrap, 1973) is
good, as is G. Jack's *Beowulf: A Student Edition* (Oxford:
Clarendon Press, 1994), but neither has the breadth of
Klaeber. A new edition by Bruce Mitchell and Fred C.
Robinson has recently been issued (Oxford: Blackwell, 1998),
with an excellent section on archaeology by Leslie Webster
of the British Museum, and some useful material on analogues and parallels. Apart from this, the volume is a basic

student edition with only limited bibliography and glossarial information.

There are many books on the poem. For a detailed treatment of many aspects of the background, see R. W. Chambers, *Beowulf: An Introduction to the Study of the Poem*, 3rd ed. with a Supplement by C. L. Wrenn (Cambridge: Cambridge University Press, 1959). The analogues are discussed and translated in *Beowulf and its Analogues*, by G. N. Garmonsway, J. Simpson, and H. E. Davidson (London: Dent, 1980). One of the most perceptive and valuable accounts of the poem's background is found in D. Whitelock, *The Audience of Beowulf* (Oxford: Clarendon Press, 1951). Among the best overall studies of the poem is A. G. Brodeur, *The Art of Beowulf* (Berkeley: University of California Press, 1959), though he does not translate his quotations; and J. R. R. Tolkien's *Beowulf: The Monsters and the Critics* (1936) belies its age. Many of my ideas derive at some removes from Tolkien's. Essays by E. G. Stanley (see *In the Foreground: Beowulf*, Woodbridge: Brewer, 1994) and F. C. Robinson (see *The Tomb of Beowulf*, Oxford: Blackwell, 1993) on the poem are many and varied, but nearly all of them are worth reading.

Anthologies of critical essays include: L. E. Nicholson, ed., *An Anthology of Beowulf Criticism* (Indiana: University of Notre Dame Press, 1964), D. K. Fry, ed., *The Beowulf Poet* (New Jersey: Twentieth Century Views, Prentice-Hall, 1968) and P. S. Baker, ed., *Basic Readings: Beowulf* (New York: Garland, 1995). By way of illustrating the diverse views on the Christian allusions in the poem, see for example in Nicholson's anthology, Blackburn (monkish redactor theory), Cabannis (liturgical formulas) and Bloomfield, Robertson and McNamee (allegory). The allegorical theory, especially as relates to the dragon, is taken to its extreme in M. E.

Goldsmith, *The Mode and Meaning of Beowulf* (London: Athlone Press, 1970). A devastating attack on the supposed paganism of the poem is C. E. Fell, 'Paganism in *Beowulf*: A Semantic Fairy-Tale', in T. Hofstra, L. A. J. R. Houwen and A. A. MacDonald, eds, *Pagans and Christians* (Groningen: *Germania Latina* II, Egbert Forsten, 1995), pp. 9–34.

Translations are very variable. E. T. Donaldson's is at the more literal end of the spectrum, but he has an excellent feel for the language. Bradley and his predecessor in Everyman, R. K. Gordon, are useful, though Bradley tends to be quirky and Gordon leaden. The Penguin translation of Alexander treads a narrow line between the bizarre and the meaningless on occasion. Burton Raffel and Gavin Bone are poets and there are some genuine poetic touches in their work. C. Kennedy, *Beowulf: The Oldest English Epic* (New York: Oxford University Press, 1940) has a good introduction and sensible translation.

# CHAPTER 8

*Genesis* is edited by George Philip Krapp in the Anglo-Saxon Poetic Records series, vol. I, *The Junius Manuscript* (New York: Columbia University Press, 1931). There is a separate edition of the part derived from the Old Saxon poem, edited by B. J. Timmer, *The Later Genesis* (Oxford: The Scrivener Press, 1948). *Juliana* is in the Exeter Book, edited by Krapp and Dobbie (see chapter 4 above) and there is a separate edition edited by Rosemary Woolf (London: Methuen's Old English Library, 1954). The Old English poem *The Lord's Prayer II* is edited by Dobbie in the Anglo-Saxon Poetic Records series, vol. VI, *The Anglo-Saxon Minor Poems*, as is the poetic version of *The Creed*. *The Seafarer* is in the Exeter Book, and is also edited by Ida Gordon (Manchester: Manchester University

Press, 1979). *The Dream of the Rood* is in the Vercelli Book, edited by Krapp in the Anglo-Saxon Poetic Records series, vol. II, and there is a very fine edition by Michael Swanton, revised ed. (Exeter: Exeter University Press, 1987). Much has been written on the poem, and Swanton's readily available bibliography will provide a guide to reading. J. M. Neale's versions of Latin hymns are available in many versions in many hymn books, but his *Mediæval Hymns and Sequences*, 3rd ed. (London: Joseph Masters, 1867) is a little gem; prose translations of the hymns of Venantius Fortunatus and others are available in Joseph Connelly, *Hymns of the Roman Liturgy* (London: Longmans, Green, 1957). A thorough study of the Ruthwell Cross, its inscriptions and history, with illustrations, has been edited by Brendan Cassidy, *The Ruthwell Cross: Papers from the Colloquium Sponsored by the Index of Christian Art ...* (Princeton: Index of Christian Art, 1992).